T0383419

Ikonen der Weltarchitektur
Icons of World Architecture

Für Sabina und Christian
For Sabina and Christian

Die Stiftung nelly rudin fördert das Buch *Ikonen der Weltarchitektur* und das Schaffen von Werner Blaser mit einem namhaften Betrag.
The nelly rudin foundation has supported the book *Icons of World Architecture* and the work of Werner Blaser with a significant financial contribution.

Buchkonzept, Text, Layout und Fotografie/Conception, Texts, Layout and Photography: Werner Blaser (ausser/except for 20, 21, 23, 24, 71, 92, 93, 141)
Satz/Typesetting: Fabio Looser, Claudia Federi, David Mäder
Lektorat/Editing: Christina Bösel, Kerstin Forster
Übersetzung/Translation: Chris Michalski
Lithografie/Lithography: Adrian Gabathuler
Druck/Printing: Heer Druck AG, Sulgen
Buchbinder/Binding: Buchbinderei Burkhardt AG, Mönchaltorf

Inhalt

Einleitung 7

Der Weg zu diesem Buch – von Adolf E. H. Jacob 9

1 NATUR 12

Im Gestalten und Bauen reflektiert sich die Natur 14
Beispiele aus und mit der Natur

2 TÓPOS 38

Beispiele davon, wie und wo das Wesentliche in Erscheinung tritt ... 40
Beispiele der Integration 46

3 SCHICHTEN 64

Das Spiel mit Stein 66
Bauwerke aus Stein 72

4 KONSTRUKTION 90

Elemente des modernen Bauens 92
Altes und Neues im Vergleich 98

5 URBILD UND ABBILD 116

Eingebung und Impulse 118
Abbild des Urbildhaften 124

6 STILLE 142

Kreative Ruhe und Schutz vor Reizüberflutung 144
Beispiele meditativer Stille 150

Rede beim Fest der Freunde zum 70. Geburtstag von Werner Blaser, ... 168
29. August 1994

Bücher von Werner Blaser 173

Kurzbiografie 175

Content

Introduction 7

How this book came about – by Adolf E. H. Jacob 9

1 NATURE 12

Nature is reflected in design and construction 14
Examples from and with nature

2 TÓPOS 38

Examples of how and where the essential is to be found ... 40
Examples of integration 46

3 Layers 64

The use of stone 66
Stone structures 72

4 Construction 90

Elements of modern construction 92
The old and new juxtaposed 98

5 ARCHETYPE AND IMAGE 116

Dictates and impulses 118
Images of the archetypical 124

6 Silence 142

Creative silence and avoiding sensory overload 144
Examples of meditative silence 150

Speech held at the celebration of Werner Blaser's 70th birthday ... 168
on 29 August 1994

Books by Werner Blaser 173

Short Biography 176

Einleitung

Mit der Zusammenstellung der vorliegenden Dokumentation versuche ich auf meine Weise der Herausforderung nachzukommen, vor die mich ein immer wiederkehrendes Ansinnen aus dem Freundeskreis stellt: Ich soll zusammenfassen und festhalten, was sich mir in meinem Suchen nach dem Wesen des Bauens und Gestaltens als gültig erwiesen hat.

Es mag sein, dass der eine oder andere, der mich mit solchen Erwartungen konfrontierte, diese mit der Vorstellung verband, ich könnte allgemeingültige Wahrheiten zum Thema Bauen und Gestalten hinterlassen, Massstäbe für gute Architektur festhalten und – Grundsätzliches aus meiner Erfahrung ableitend – Lehrsätze formulieren. Doch es gibt keine Rezepte für gutes Bauen und Gestalten. Wir können über das Kreative nicht verfügen, und es lässt sich nicht in Formeln fassen. Aber es begegnet uns in Beispielen.

Mein Buch will nichts anderes, als die Begegnung mit solchen Beispielen zu dokumentieren. Die Gliederung des Buches lässt erkennen, welche Aspekte für mich als Basis guten Bauens bedeutsam geworden sind:

Natur. In der Begegnung mit der finnischen Landschaft mit ihren Wäldern und Seen erschloss sich mir unter dem Einfluss von Alvar Aalto die Bedeutung, welche die Natur in der Architektur hat.

Tópos. Gebaut wird immer an einem konkreten Ort. Er bildet im unmittelbaren Sinn die Basis des Bauwerks. Der Tópos stellt die Herausforderung dar, auf welche die Architektur die beste Antwort zu finden bemüht ist. Wahre Architektur lässt Tópos und Bauwerk in einem Baukunstwerk eins werden.

Schichtung. Gutes Bauen bewährt sich beim Umgang mit dem Baustoff Stein. Sorgfältige Schichtung ist der Schmuck eines Steinbauwerks. Sie ist ein Ornament, das im Bauwerk enthalten ist und ihm nicht hinzugefügt werden muss – gleichsam ein Ornament ohne Ornament.

Konstruktion. Für Ludwig Mies van der Rohe bildeten die neuen wissenschaftlichen und technischen Möglichkeiten der Moderne die eigentliche Voraussetzung für die Baukunst unserer Zeit. Wie Materialien und Produkte dieser Zeit – als Einzelteile – in den Gesamtaufbau integriert und zu einem Baukunstwerk der Moderne werden, dafür bietet sein Werk die besten Beispiele. Mies van der Rohe war mein Lehrmeister.

Urbild und Abbild. Wenn wir ganz bei der Sache sind, uns in ihr verlieren, werden im Kraftfeld des Kreativen Urbilder aktiviert, die in diesem Kraftfeld enthalten sind. Sie lassen in unserer Fantasie neue und alte Abbilder des Urbildhaften auftauchen und verbinden uns mit den Wurzeln unserer Kultur. Ohne diese Verbindung wird Neues nicht zur Blüte getrieben.

Introduction

With the compilation of the following documentation I have tried in my own way to respond to the challenge that has been posed to me again and again by friends of mine. These individuals have requested that I document and describe what in my search for the essence of construction and design I have come to feel is most important.

It is possible that one or two of the friends who came to me with this request hoped that I could set down general truths about construction and design, define standards for good architecture and formulate rules or tenets based on fundamental principles derived from my experiences. But there is no recipe for good construction and design. We have no control over creativity and it cannot be expressed in terms of a formula. Yet we can find examples of it.

My book strives to do nothing but document encounters with such examples. The book's structure communicates which aspects I believe are the basis for good construction:

Nature. The influence of Alvar Aalto and my impressions of the Finnish landscape with its many forests and lakes made clear to me just how important a role nature plays in architecture.

Tópos. A building is always constructed in a specific place. This location serves as the foundation of the structure in a direct sense. The tópos presents the challenge that the architecture must respond to in the best possible way. True architecture brings tópos and structure together in a single work of construction.

Layers. Good construction comes to light with the use of stone as a building material. Careful layering is the main adornment of a stone structure. It is an ornament contained within the structure itself, not one that has to be added an ornament without ornamentation.

Construction. For Ludwig Mies van der Rohe the new scientific and technological potential of modernity was fundamental to the architecture of our age. His work serves as the best example of how the materials and products of the modern era can be integrated into a structure as individual elements and formed into a contemporary architectural work. Mies van der Rohe was my mentor and teacher.

Archetype and Image. When we are completely immersed in something, lose ourselves in it, archetypes are activated in a creative aura, archetypes that are contained within this aura. They call forth new and old images in our imaginations and connect us with the roots of our culture. Without this kind of connection new creations cannot come to fruition.

Stille. Mein Wissen um die Bedeutung der Stille verdanke ich dem Vorbild meines Vaters und dem meines Lehrmeisters Mies van der Rohe. Mein Studienaufenthalt in Japan und die Begegnungen mit der Zenkultur haben dieses Wissen vertieft und ins Zentrum meines Bewusstseins gerückt. Auf die Bedeutung von Stille weist das Gestaltungsprinzip «less is more» ebenso hin wie das der Meditation entnommene Wissen um die Fülle, die aus der Leere kommt.

Zu jedem einzelnen der sechs Themen, die der Dokumentation ihre Gliederung verleihen, ist eine Bildfolge gewählt. Diese teilt sich, soweit möglich, jeweils wie folgt auf: Zuerst werden sechs Bilder zum jeweiligen Thema gezeigt, die meinem unmittelbaren Werkbereich entnommen sind. Wo es mir hilfreich schien, habe ich noch ein die jeweilige Thematik unterstreichendes weiteres Bild beigefügt, das nicht meinem Werkbereich zugehört. An diese ersten sechs oder mehr Bilder schliessen sich achtzehn Bilder vorbildlicher Beispiele aus aller Welt an.

Mit dem, was ich gesehen und in Bildern festgehalten hatte, pflegte ich meine Freunde zu konfrontieren und sie damit zum Mitdenken und zum Gespräch anzuregen. Allen, die sich an diesen Gesprächen beteiligten, bleibe ich in Dankbarkeit verbunden, was das vorliegende Buch zum Ausdruck bringen will. Besonders zu danken habe ich Adolf E. H. Jacob, der mir seit 1947 Gesprächspartner und Freund ist. Im Gespräch mit ihm hat auch das vorliegende Buch seine Gestalt gewonnen – ein Prozess, den er im Folgenden beschreibt.

Silence. I owe my knowledge of the meaning of silence to my role model, my father, and to my mentor, Mies van der Rohe. The time I spent studying in Japan and my encounters with Zen culture deepened this knowledge and pushed it towards the center of my thinking. The design principle "less is more" demonstrates the importance of silence, as does the knowledge gained from meditation on the great abundance found in emptiness.

For each of the six themes around which the book has been structured a series of images has been chosen and in most cases arranged as follows: first six images are shown from my direct working environment to illustrate the particular subject. Whenever it seemed helpful I have added an additional image not from my immediate working environment. To supplement these first six or more images, 18 images of exemplary works from all over the world are reprinted.

In the past I would often seek out my friends and show them what I had seen and documented in my pictures in order to inspire them to reflect on and discuss different subjects. I owe everything that this book attempts to express to all those who took part in these conversations, and I am grateful to them. I would especially like to thank Adolf E. H. Jacob, who has been a conversational partner and friend of mine since 1947. This book has come into being in the course of discussions with him – a process that he describes in the following pages.

Der Weg zu diesem Buch
von Adolf E. H. Jacob

Vor einigen Jahren, anlässlich des 70. Geburtstages von Werner Blaser wurde ich von seinem Sohn Christian W. Blaser eingeladen, vor dem grossen Kreis der Freunde die Festrede zu halten und den Toast auf den Jubilar auszubringen.

Erst zögerte ich, diese ehrenvolle Einladung anzunehmen, weil ich ja nur als Freund reden konnte, aber der Auffassung war, es sollte bei einem solchen Anlass nicht nur das Freundschaftliche zur Sprache kommen. Ich hätte mir gewünscht, dass an einem solchen Tag auch das Werk gewürdigt würde, mit dem der Jubilar sich weltweit als Wegweiser zu guter Architektur verdient gemacht hat und durch das er auch hierzulande zum Wegbereiter dafür wurde, dass da und dort, bei uns und in unserer Nachbarschaft, Beispiele guten Bauens entstehen konnten.

Da ich aber weder Architekt oder Kunstwissenschaftler noch Basler bin, hielt ich mich nicht für kompetent, in meiner Rede über das Freundschaftliche hinaus auch das Werk des Jubilars und seine Bedeutung für unsere Region zur Sprache zu bringen. Es war mir aber eine Freude und Ehre, die Festrede halten zu dürfen. Deshalb musste sich meine Rede mit der Würdigung des Persönlichen begnügen.

Viele aus dem Freundeskreis von Werner Blaser sind oder waren auf völlig anderen Gebieten als dem des Bauens und der Gestaltung tätig. Durch die Begegnung mit Werner Blaser und seinen Arbeiten lernten sie auf diesem Gebiet aber sehen und unterscheiden. Auch ich gehöre zu diesen Laien.

Da uns die Buchpublikationen von Werner Blaser die Augen öffnen konnten für das Wahre und Schöne von Bauwerken und auch andere Werke moderner Produktgestaltung, stellten wir ihm immer wieder Fragen nach den Grundsätzen und Massstäben, die allgemein für gute Architektur und gutes Design gelten. Wir wünschten uns eine Verdeutlichung und Zusammenfassung dessen, was er uns in seinen zahlreichen Veröffentlichungen gezeigt hatte.

Um unserem Wunsch nachzukommen, stellte Werner Blaser die hier vorliegende Fotodokumentation zusammen. Er gliederte diese Dokumentation in sechs für das Bauen wesentliche Aspekte. Mit den fotografischen Bildbeispielen zu jedem dieser sechs Aspekte will uns Werner Blaser gleichsam darüber ins Bild setzen, was aus seiner Sicht zur Basis des Bauens gehört. Da ich wohl derjenige bin, der Werner Blaser am meisten zur Veröffentlichung einer solchen Dokumentation gedrängt hat, hat er mich eingeladen, mit ihm zusammen die von ihm entworfenen Bildlegenden zu den einzelnen Beispielen kritisch durchzugehen und mich am Versuch zu beteiligen, für die Wahrheit, über die uns das einzelne Bildbeispiel ins Bild setzt, auch eine sprachliche Aussage zu finden.

Bei diesem gemeinsamen Suchen ging es also darum, für das, was ein Bild eben nur bildhaft vermitteln kann, soweit möglich eine entsprechende Übersetzung in die Sprache zu finden oder wenigstens darum, mit Worten die Richtung anzudeuten, in die das Bild weist.

How this book came about
by Adolf E. H. Jacob

Several years ago, on the occasion of Werner Blaser's 70th birthday, I was invited by his son, Christian W. Blaser, to give a speech and offer a toast to the guest of honor before his many friends.

At first I hesitated to accept this great distinction, because I felt that while I would only be able to speak as a friend, on such an important occasion more than just the aspects of friendship should be addressed. It was my wish that tribute be paid to the work that had made the guest of honor well known all over the world as an ambassador for good architecture, and that had shaped his reputation in this country as a pioneer who had shown that our and our neighbors' houses could become prototypes of superior construction.

Since I am neither an architect nor an art scholar nor even a resident of Basel, I didn't feel like I had the necessary expertise to go beyond the aspects of our friendship and express the importance of the honored guest's work and its significance for our region. And yet it was such great a joy and distinction to be permitted to give this speech that I had to content myself with an homage to his personal qualities.

Many individuals from Werner Blaser's circle of friends are or were active in fields quite distant from construction or design. Yet through their encounters with him and his work they learned to see and understand this subject. I am one of those laymen.

As the books by Werner Blaser opened our eyes to some of the true and beautiful elements of architectural creations and of other works of modern product design, we often asked him questions about the principles and proportions upon which good architecture and design are based. We hoped that he would provide a clear summary of that which he had demonstrated to us in his numerous publications.

In order to satisfy this wish of ours Werner Blaser has put together this photographic documentation. He has structured the work around six components essential to all construction. With the photographs that illustrate each of these components, the author has attempted to pictorially demonstrate what he believes to be the fundamental aspects of construction.

Since I am apparently the individual who urged Werner Blaser most emphatically to publish this documentation, he asked me to critically review with him the picture captions that he had drafted and to assist him in attempting to find the correct description for the truth that each individual picture reveals. We wanted to find the right translation into words of that which an image can only visually communicate – or at least words that could point in the same direction as the image.

Together the image and the caption should reveal the principle, to which the architectural example bears witness. "There is no recipe for good construction and design," says Werner Blaser. "We have no control over creativity and it cannot be expressed in terms of a formula. Yet we see it in various examples." To this I would like to add: in encountering and examining these examples our own critical faculty is able to develop. Through positive and

So sollten Bild und Bildlegende gemeinsam den Grundsatz erkennbar werden lassen, von dem das gezeigte Beispiel zeugt. «Es gibt keine Rezepte für gutes Bauen und Gestalten», sagt Werner Blaser. Und weiter: «Wir können über das Kreative nicht verfügen, und es lässt sich nicht in Formeln fassen. Aber es begegnet uns in Beispielen.» Und dem möchte ich hinzufügen: In der Begegnung mit Beispielen und im Umgang mit ihnen bildet sich das Urteilsvermögen. An positiven und negativen Beispielen wie denen des Wahren, Schönen und Edlen und denen des Gegenteils differenzieren und kultivieren sich unsere Gefühle, aus denen unser wertendes Denken sein Urteilsvermögen schöpft.

Mit der vorliegenden Beispielsammlung ist Werner Blaser unserem Drängen nachgekommen, zusammenzufassen und festzuhalten, was sich ihm in seinem Suchen nach dem Wesen des Bauens und Gestaltens als gültig erwiesen hat.

Vor über zehn Jahren habe ich den Mangel empfunden, dass mir für meine Rede zum 70. Geburtstag die Kompetenz fehlte, neben der Person auch das Werk des Jubilars zu würdigen. Heute sehe ich das anders: Das Werk ist das, was die Person geleistet hat. Aber die Person ist mehr als ihre Leistung. Das Werk ist zwar die Spur, die die Person hinterlässt, aber die Spur ist nicht die Person selbst. Die Wahrheit darüber, wer diese Person aber ist, leuchtet erst in der Begegnung von Mensch zu Mensch auf.

Wer Werner Blaser ist, versuchte ich damals in der konkreten Situation des Festes der Freunde, als Festrede und als Toast auf den Jubilar zur Sprache zu bringen.

Mit der vorliegenden Bilddokumentation können wir die Spuren lesen, die Werner Blasers beruflichen Weg markieren. Die Würdigung seines Werkes fehlte mir damals beim Fest der Freunde. Nun, wo die vorliegende Bilddokumentation dieses Werk würdigt, indem sie zeigt, worum es darin geht, bedarf sie der Ergänzung – der Ergänzung durch das, was in der Person zu suchen ist, die hinter dem Werk steht.

Was ich damals hierzu in der konkreten Situation des Festes der Freunde zur Sprache bringen wollte, ist immer noch gültig, und ich wüsste es heute kaum besser zu sagen. Deshalb und weil das vorliegende Buch so an der besonderen Atmosphäre der Festversammlung der Freunde von 1994 anknüpfen kann, gebe ich hier das, was zur Person zu sagen ist, die hinter diesem Werk steht, ganz in der Form von damals wieder, nämlich als Rede zum Fest der Freunde und als Toast auf Werner Blaser. Sie ist am Schluss des Buches wiedergegeben und gilt auch heute noch.

negative examples of the true, beautiful and noble – as well as the very opposite – our feelings, from which our critical thinking and judgment spring, are cultivated.

With this collection of architectural examples Werner Blaser has fulfilled our wish that he put together a collection and documentation of the aspects that in his search for the essence of construction and design he has come to feel are most important.

Over ten years ago, when I delivered my speech on the occasion of Werner Blaser's 70th birthday, I did not feel that I had the necessary expertise to pay tribute to him as both a man and architect. Now I see that differently: Werner Blaser's work is his great achievement, but he is more than this achievement. The work may be the traces that a man leaves behind, but these traces are not the man himself. We only learn who this man truly is when we meet him face to face.

Back then, at that celebration with friends, I tried to express in my speech and toast just who Werner Blaser is.

In this photographic documentation we now see the traces that Werner Blaser has left behind on his profession. At that celebration I was unable to pay proper homage to his work. Now that this photographic documentation pays homage to his work by illustrating what this work is about, something is still lacking – an explanation of the man behind the work.

What I wanted to express at that celebration with friends is as true now as ever, and I don't think I could say it much better than I did back then. For this reason – and because this book has so much to do with the special atmosphere of that celebratory gathering among friends in 1994 – I have included here what must be said about the man behind the work the same way I expressed it then, as a speech and toast to Werner Blaser. The text is included at the end of this book. It expresses ideas and emotions that still ring true to me many years later.

Unterwegs zwischen Bestehendem und Neuem.

Biografisches, dargestellt an Beispielen dessen, was ich gesehen, worüber ich reflektiert, was ich erarbeitet habe.

Werner Blase

Striking a balance between that which has come before and that which is new.
Biographical considerations as they relate to the subjects of my reflections and creations.

1 NATUR
NATURE

Im Gestalten und Bauen reflektiert sich die Natur

Nature is reflected in design and construction

Seelandschaft in Hämeenlinna, Finnland / Streckenverbindung in Holz (Collage des Autors, 1955–1975).

Sea landscape in Hämeenlinna, Finland / Wood section joint (collage by the author, 1955–1975).

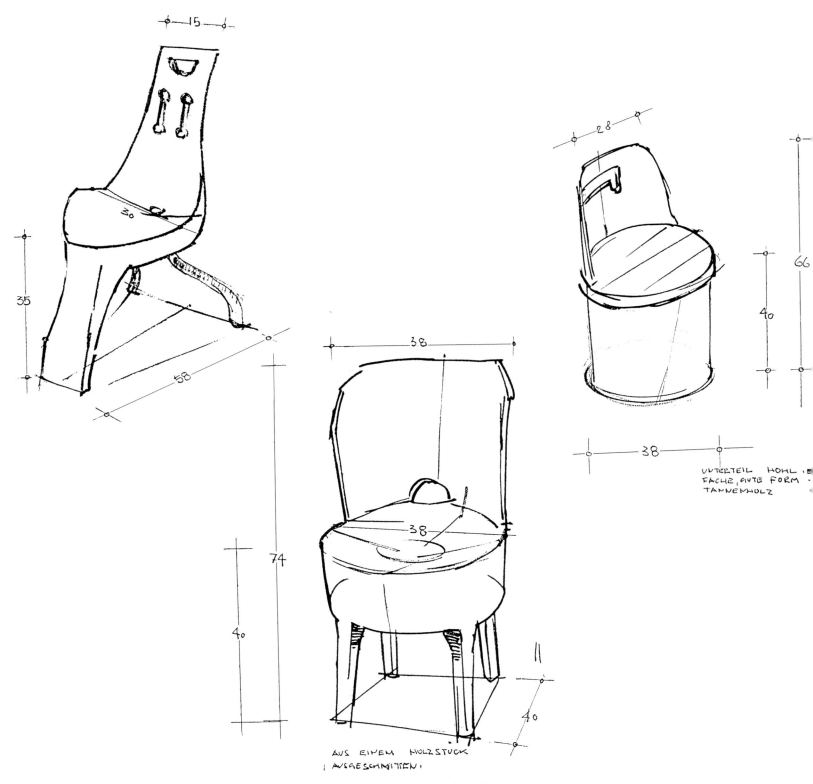

Aufnahmeskizzen aus skandinavischen Freilichtmuseen (Werner Blaser, 1949) – Gewachsene Elemente bestimmen die Gestaltung.

Sketches from Scandinavian open air museums (Werner Blaser, 1949) – Highly advanced components determine the design.

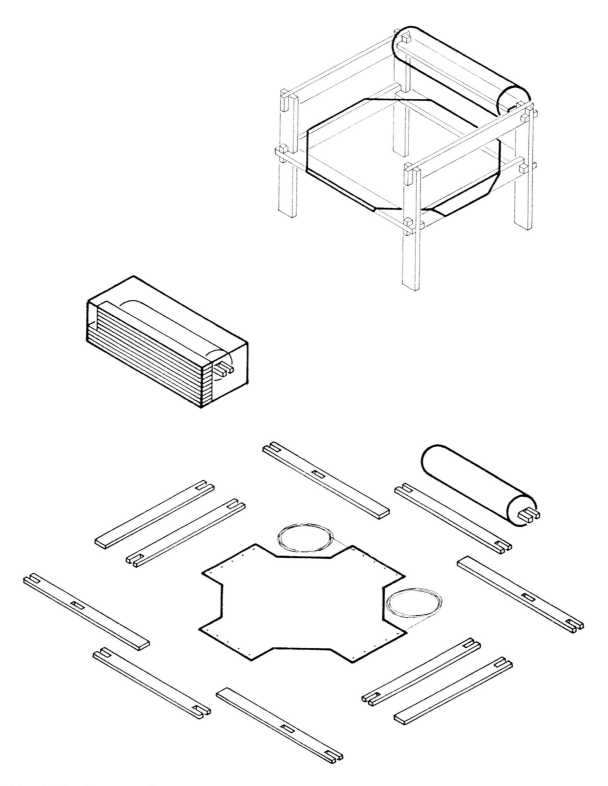

Fugungsprinzip aus drei Stabelementen (Werner Blaser, 1955–1975) – Die formgleichen Stabelemente bewirken das Entstehen eines vielfältigen Möbelprogramms.

Joint concept with three peg components (Werner Blaser, 1955–1975) – The similarly shaped peg components yield an extensive number of furniture designs.

Holzstapel in Finnland – Spiel des Modularen im anonymen Objekt.

Pile of wood in Finland – Interplay of modular units in an anonymous structure.

Steckspiel aus Stäben von quadratischem Querschnitt (Werner Blaser, 1956–1965) – Wechselspiel des Gleichen in der Kombination.

Stacking game with rectangular wood pieces (Werner Blaser, 1956–1965) – Interplay of identical components in combination.

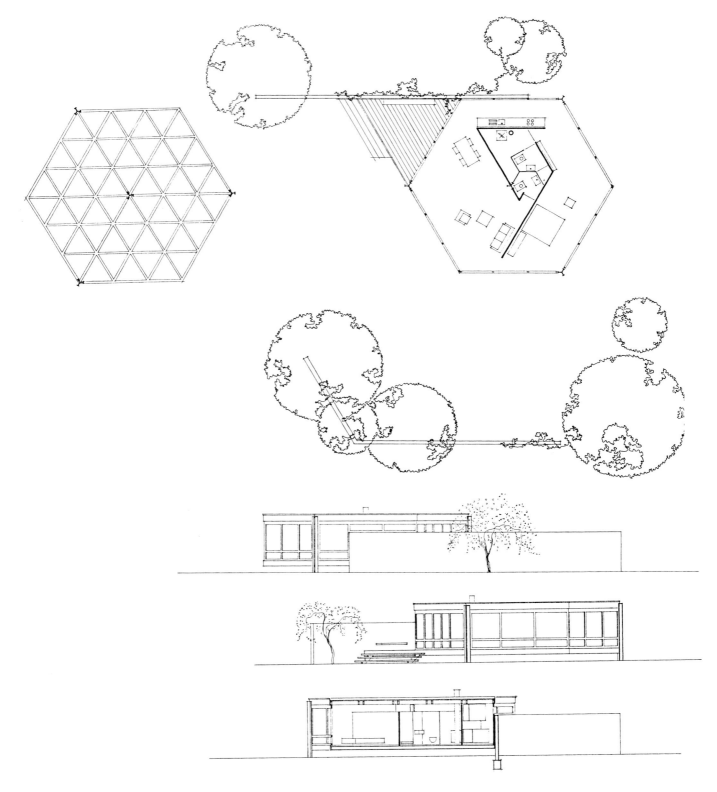

Sechseckhäuser aus Holzskelett (Projektentwicklung Werner Blaser, 1968) – Konzentration auf das Elementare.

Six-sided wooden frame houses (project development: Werner Blaser, 1968) – Focus on the elemental.

Sechseckhaus aus Holzskelett, Schweizer Jura (Werner Blaser, 1972) – Wechselwirkung zwischen Natur und Bauwerk.

Six-sided wooden frame house, Jura Mountains, Switzerland (Werner Blaser, 1972) – Interplay between nature and structure.

Naturform und plastisches Experiment (Alvar Aalto, 1929–1933) – Gestaltgebung der Dynamik der Natur nachempfunden.

Natural form and plastic experiment (Alvar Aalto, 1929–1933) – Design based on the dynamics of nature.

Experiment «Spaltung und Biegung» (Alvar Aalto, 1929–1933) – Technisches und ästhetisches Formen bis zur plastischen Holzgestaltung.

"Division and Bending", experiment (Alvar Aalto, 1929–1933) – Technical and aesthetic forming results in a plastic wood design.

Waldlandschaft in Finnland – Bäume bilden den organischen Raum Wald.

Forest landscape in Finland – Trees shape the organic space of the forest.

Finnischer Pavillon auf der Weltausstellung in New York (Alvar Aalto, 1938–1939) – In der wellenförmigen Wand bleibt das Organische gegenwärtig.

Finnish pavilion at the World's Fair in New York (Alvar Aalto, 1938–1939) – In the undulating wall the organic element is given emphasis.

Seenlandschaft Punkaharju in Finnland – Biotop als Ur-Natur.

Punkaharju sea landscape in Finland – Biotope as elemental nature.

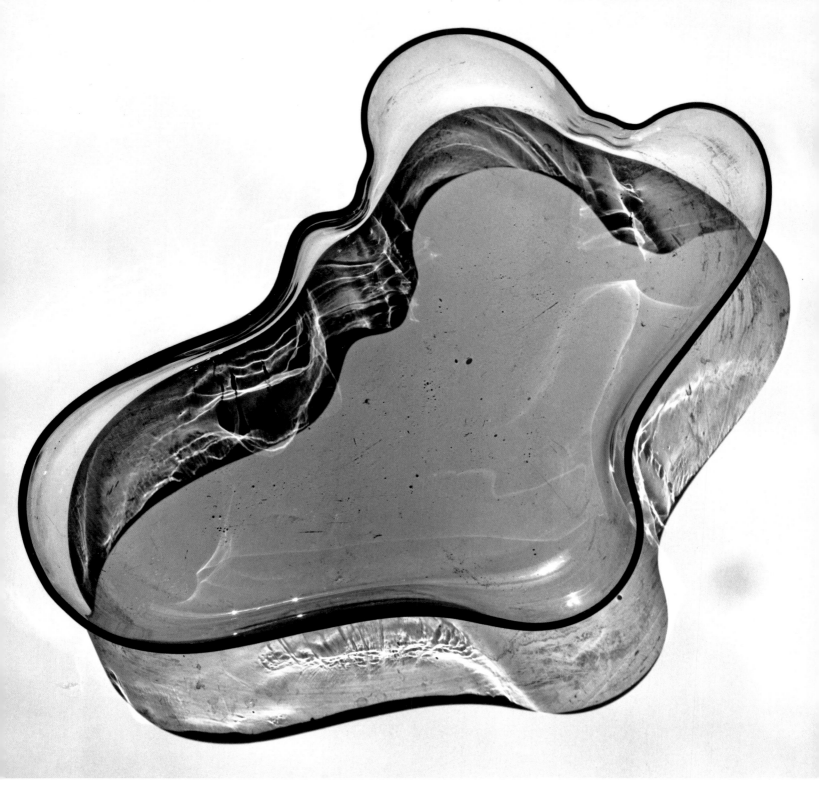

Organische iittala-Vase (Alvar und Aino Aalto, um 1937) – Hommage an die Natur.

Organic iittala vase (Alvar and Aino Aalto, ca. 1937) – Homage to nature.

Palm House Bicton Gardens in Budleigh Salterton, England (D. und E. Bailey, 1843) – Das Palmblatt inspiriert zur Konstruktion.

The Palm House, Bicton Gardens in Budleigh Salterton, England (D. and E. Bailey, 1843) – The palm leaf inspires the construction.

Palm House Bicton Gardens – Pflanzenartiges Gerippe mit Glaswaben.

The Palm House, Bicton Gardens – Plant-like frame with glass honeycombs.

Great Conservatory, Syon House Park in London (Charles Fowler, 1820–1827) – Bauen als organisches Konstruieren.

Great Conservatory, Syon House Park, London (Charles Fowler, 1820–1827) – Construction as organic fabrication.

Great Conservatory – Natürliche Einheit von Material und Konstruktion.

Great Conservatory – Natural unity unity of material and structure.

Viktoriahaus in Basel (1898, Rekonstruktion 1996) – Die nach der Königin Victoria benannte Seerose «victoria amazonica» misst bis zu zwei Meter.

Viktoriahaus in Basel (1898, reconstructed 1996) – The water lily named after Queen Victoria, *victoria amazonica,* extends up to two meters.

Botanischer Garten Kibble Palace, Glasgow (John Kibble, 1865–1873) – Weitumspannende Konstruktion.

Kibble Palace Botanic Gardens, Glasgow (John Kibble, 1865–1873) – Expansive construction.

Bauernhaus in Kiew – Eine Astgabelung weitet die Tragfähigkeit aus.

Farmhouse in Kiev – Branching increases the load capacity.

Stansted Airport in London (Norman Foster, 1989–1991) – Prinzip der Astgabelung im Säulensystem.

Stansted Airport in London (Norman Foster, 1989–1991) – Principle of branching in the column system.

Gare TGV de Satolas, Lyon (Santiago Calatrava, 1989–1994) – Erschaffen nach der Bewegung eines zum Flug ansetzenden Vogels.

Gare TGV de Satolas, Lyon (Santiago Calatrava, 1989–1994) – Conceived after the motion of a bird taking off.

Gare TGV de Satolas – Das Knochengerüst des «Vogels» bildet den Raum.

Gare TGV de Satolas – The skeleton of the "bird" shapes the space.

Zwergpalme aus Sizilien – Strukturelemente in ihrer Auffächerung.

Chamaerops from Sicily – Structural elements opening out like fans.

Vorhalle, Hauptbahnhof Köln (Stefan Polónyi, 1985–1991) – Gebündelte Pfeiler fächern das Bogenwerk auf.

Front hall, Cologne train station (Stefan Polónyi, 1985–1991) – A bundle of arrows fans out to create the arch.

2 Tópos

Tópos

Der Ort der Architektur, wo sich die Vielfalt und das Gegensätzliche zur Einheit des Ganzen verbinden. Analysierendes Betrachten stellt Fragen nach dem Sinnvollen und Gültigen beim Bauen.

The place in architecture where diversity and opposition are unified in the composition. Analytical observation poses questions regarding meaning and truth in construction

Traditioneller japanischer Schirm aus Bambus / Lagerhalle in Raumfachwerk (Collage des Autors, 1970–1971).

Traditional Japanese bamboo umbrella / Framework structure of a warehouse (collage by the author, 1970–1971).

Wegkreuz bei Assisi – Wo sich Vertikale und Horizontale schneiden, lässt sich erkennen, ob das Zusammenspiel von Baukonstruktion und Bauelement «echt» ist. Tankraupen dienten hier als Bauelement.

Roadside cross near Assisi – Where the vertical and horizontal meet it is possible to see whether the interplay of structural design and material is "true". Here tank crawlers were used as the building material.

Kreuzfussverbindung als plastisches Experiment (Werner Blaser, 1952–1962) – Eine handwerkliche Spielart der Kunst der Fuge.

Crossed-leg joint as plastic experiment (Werner Blaser, 1952–1962) – A hand crafted variant of the art of connecting elements.

Traditionelles Appenzellerhaus in Trogen (17.–18. Jahrhundert) – Eine Vorstufe der *curtain wall*

Traditional Appenzeller house in Trogen, Switzerland (17th 18th century) – An early version of the curtain wall.

Kinderdorf Müllheim, Baden-Württemberg (Werner Blaser, 1966–1967) – Das Ganze reflektiert das konstruktive Detail und umgekehrt.

Müllheim Children's Village (Werner Blaser, 1966–1967) – The entire construction reflects the structural details and vice-versa.

Raumkreuz aus sieben Kuben in Plexiglas (Werner Blaser, 1960) – Linien und Flächen spiegeln sich im Licht.

Intersection of seven plexiglass cubes (Werner Blaser, 1960) – Lines and surfaces are reflected in the light.

Demontables Pavillonsystem der CIBA-Photochemie in Köln (Werner Blaser, 1963) – Decken- und Bodenraster als wechselseitiges Spiegelbild.

Demountable pavilion system for CIBA-Photochemie in Cologne (Werner Blaser, 1963) – Roof and floor grid as two-way reflection.

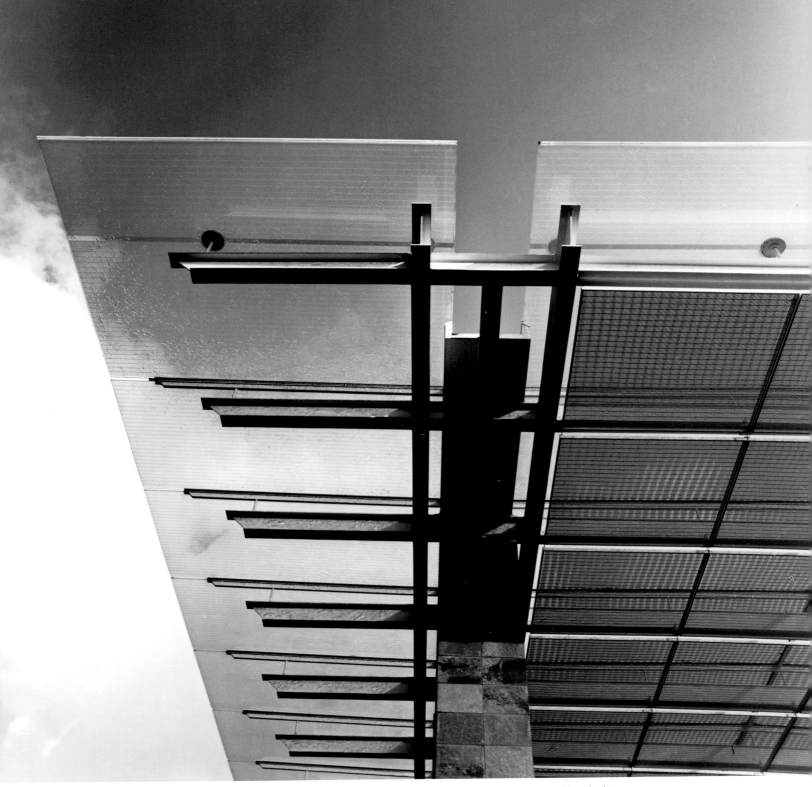

Fondation Beyeler, Museum im Berowerpark, Riehen bei Basel (Renzo Piano, 1991–1997) – Dachsegel als der Ort, wo das Tageslicht in das Bauwerk integriert ist.

Fondation Beyeler, Museum in Berowerpark, Riehen bei Basel, Switzerland (Renzo Piano, 1991–1997) – The roof sail as the point where daylight is integrated into the building.

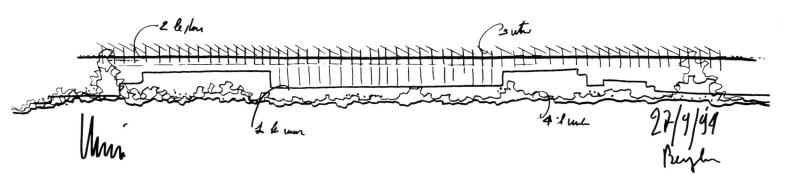

Fondation Beyeler – Ein Ort, an dem Licht, Landschaft und Funktion in jene Gültigkeit einfliessen, die wir mit dem Begriff Architektur umschreiben (Skizze Renzo Piano 1994).

Fondation Beyeler – A place where light, landscape and function flow together into a single force that can be described as architecture (Renzo Piano sketch, 1994).

Pavillon im Berowerpark – Zusammenspiel von Umgebung und Gebäude.

Pavilion in Berowerpark – Building interacting with its environs.

Fondation Beyeler – Integration der Architektur in die Gegebenheiten von Ort, Landschaft, Natur, Geschichte.

Fondation Beyeler – Integration of the architecture in a specific location, landscape, nature, history.

Renzo Piano Building Workshop in Genua, 1969–1986 – Vegetation im Atelier mit transparentem Dach und Sicht aufs Meer – Ohne das Bauwerk näher zu kennen, lässt uns sein Anblick erfassen, was der Architekt wil

Renzo Piano Building Workshop in Genoa, 1986–1969 – Vegetation in the studio with transparent roof and a view of the sea – Without closer knowledge of the construction the look of the building alone communicate to us the architect's intention.

Renzo Piano Building Workshop – Lichtführung als technische Notwendigkeit in der Glasdachkonstruktion.

Renzo Piano Building Workshop – Use of light as a technical necessity in glass roof construction.

Haustypen auf der Insel Stromboli, Italien – Schlichtheit des Kubus. Durch die Formwiederholung in den Nachbarbauten entsteht ein Synergieeffekt.

Variety of houses on the island of Stromboli, Italy – Simplicity of the cube. The repetition of forms in neighboring structures creates a synergy effect.

Villa Savoye in Poissy bei Paris (Le Corbusier, 1928–1931) – Wirkung des Kubischen.

Villa Savoye in Poissy near Paris (Le Corbusier, 1928–1931) – Effect of the cubistic form.

Weinrebenkulturen auf der Insel Stromboli, Italien – Gitterraster für die Pflanzen.

Grape vines on the island of Stromboli, Italy – Grid work for the plants.

Bauhaus Dessau (Walter Gropius, 1926) – Fassadenraster, vor die Konstruktion gestellt.

Bauhaus Dessau (Walter Gropius, 1926) – Façade grid attached to the front of the construction.

Holzfassaden der Casas de las Galerías in La Coruña, Spanien (um 1830) – Glasvorbauten als Wintergarten und Ausgleichszone für Wärme und Kälte.

Wood façades of the Casas de las Galerías in La Coruña, Spain (ca. 1830) – Glass front buildings as winter garden and space for the equalization of warm and cold.

Holzfensterarchitektur in Tomsk, Sibirien (19. Jahrhundert) – Ornamente an vorgesetzten Fenstern und Dachkreuz.

Wood window architecture in Tomsk, Siberia (19th century) – Ornamentation on the protruding windows and rooftop cross.

Maiensäss im Verzascatal, Schweiz – In die Landschaft integrierte Einheit von Material und Gestalt.

Maiensäss (mountain farmhouse) in the Verzasca valley, Switzerland – Material and design integrated into the landscape.

Taliesin East in Spring Green, Wisconsin (Frank Lloyd Wright, um 1950) – Das Dach als Teil eines gewachsenen Hangs.

Taliesin East in Spring Green, Wisconsin (Frank Lloyd Wright, ca. 1950) – The roof as part of a steep slope.

Ponte degli Alpini in Bassano, Italien (Andrea Palladio, 1567–1569, Rekonstruktion 1957) – Mit Kufen verbundene, transparente Holzverkleidungen schützen die Brückenpfeiler und ergänzen die Gesamtkonstruktion.

Ponte degli Alpini in Bassano, Italy (Andrea Palladio, 1567–1569, reconstructed in 1957) – The transparent wood casing joined with runners protects the bridge pillars and complements the entire construction.

Saanebrücke bei Gümmenen, Bern – Die Einkleidung schützt die Konstruktion.

Bridge over the Saane River near Gümmenen, Bern, Switzerland – The exterior sheathing protects the structure.

Zisterzienserabtei Fontenay im Burgund, Frankreich (1139–1147) – Die klare Dachkonstruktion wölbt sich über dem Meditationsraum.

The Cistercian Abbey of Fontenay in Burgundy, France (1139–1147) – The clear roof construction arches over the meditation room.

Liverpool Station, London (um 1830) – Die Konstruktion überspannt den Grossraum.

Liverpool Station, London (ca. 1830) – The structure spans over an enormous space.

3 SCHICHTEN
LAYERS

Schichtung und Baugestalt – Stein auf Stein zu Statik und Ästhetik

Layering and construction design – stone on stone in the molding of statics and aesthetics

Mondtore im Kaiserpalast, Peking / Friedhof Brion bei Treviso von Carlo Scarpa, 1970–1975 (Collage des Autors).

Moon Gates in the Imperial Palace, Beijing / Brion Cemetery outside Treviso, Italy by Carlo Scarpa, 1970–1975 (collage by the author).

Findlinge im Val Bavona, Schweiz – Welten des Steins.

Boulders in Val Bavona, Switzerland – Kingdom of stone.

Spielen im Valle Maggia, Schweiz – Die Steine sind mein Auto.

Playing in Valle Maggia, Switzerland – The stones are my car.

Bodenmosaik. Der Westliche Gartentempel Hsi-yuan-ssu (1635) in Soochow, China – Paviment mit Motiven aus Bachkieseln.

Floor mosaic. The Western Garden Temple Hsi-yuan-ssu (1635) in Suzhou, China – Floor pattern with images formed from pebbles.

Oktogonales Steinmuster, Barfüsserplatz, Basel (Werner Blaser, 1976) – Transformation des Paviments in Kopfsteinpflaster.

Octagonal stone pattern, Barfüsserplatz, Basel (Werner Blaser, 1976) – Transformation of the mosaic into cobblestones.

Kreuz in einer Steinmauer bei Kiew – Das Kreuz ist Bestandteil der Schichtung.

Cross in a stone wall near Kiev – The cross is built into the layers of stone.

Kreuz im Verband der Backsteinwand, Friedhof Bromhübel, Arlesheim, Schweiz (Werner Blaser, 1967–1969) – Ornament ohne Ornament.

Cross in the bracing of the brick wall, Bromhübel Cemetery, Arlesheim, Switzerland (Werner Blaser, 1967–1969) – Ornamentation without ornamentation.

Steingefüge im Village des Bories in Gordes, Vaucluse, Frankreich (etwa 18. Jahrhundert) – Der Stein als erstes Modul des Bauens.

Stone framework in the Village des Bories in Gordes, Vaucluse, France (ca. 18th century) – Stone as the first module of construction.

Hofhaussiedlung Fredensborg, Dänemark (Jørn Utzon, 1962–1963) – Umzäunung / Einfassung.

Houses with courtyards in Fredensborg, Denmark (Jørn Utzon, 1962–1963) – Fencing / trimming.

Steingehege auf den Aran-Inseln, Irland – Stein auf Stein und nichts als Steine.

Stone enclosure on the Aran Islands, Ireland – Stone on stone and nothing but stone.

3 Layers Uses of stone

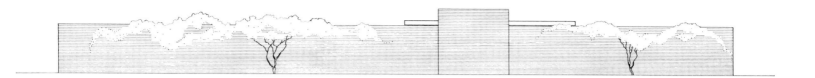

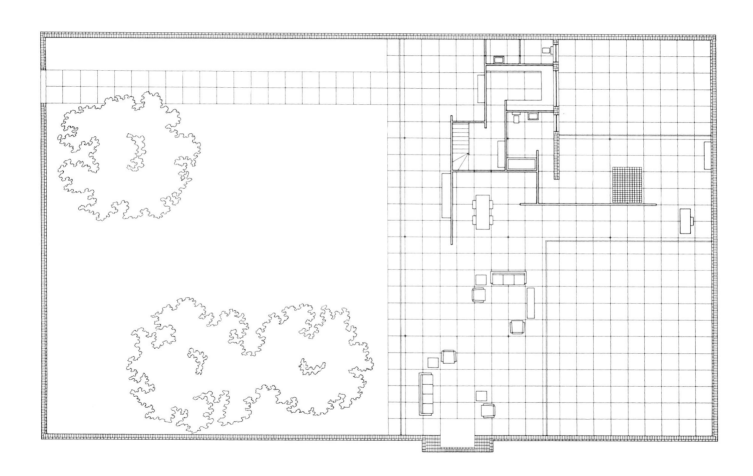

Steinbauprojekt mit drei Höfen (Mies van der Rohe, 1934) – Der Stein als Modul.

Stone construction project with three courtyards (Mies van der Rohe, 1934) – Stone as module.

Sichtmauerwerk in Barrington Hills, Illinois (John C. Heinrich, 1970) – Modulation im Backsteinverbund.

Fairfaced masonry in Barrington Hills, Illinois (John C. Heinrich, 1970) – Modulation in the brick joints.

Atrium-Siedlung nahe dem Hyde Park, Chicago (Yau-chun Wong, 1961) – Zugang von aussen zum abgeschirmten Inneren.

Houses with atrium near Hyde Park, Chicago (Yau-chun Wong, 1961) – Exterior access to the protected interior.

Detail eines Maiensässes in Brione, Val Verzasca, Schweiz, heute als Wohnstätte genutzt (Peter Degen) – Beispiel für Umfunktionieren und Erhalten.

Detail of a *Maiensäss* (mountain farmhouse) in Brione, Val Verzasca, Switzerland, now used as a residence (Peter Degen) – Example of conversion and preservation.

Maiensäss in Brione im Val Verzasca – Bis heute Fortbestehendes.

Maiensäss in Brione, Val Verzasca – Still standing.

Astronomisches Observatorium Guangxing Tai in Dengfeng, China (1279) – Mass und Masse in Symmetrie.

Guangxing Tai Observatory in Dengfeng, China (1279) – Dimensions and mass in symmetry.

Sikandra-Grabanlage von Mogul Akbar, Indien (1615) – Das Tor erschafft eine Innenwelt.

Tomb of Akbar the Mughal emperor in Sikandar, India (1615) – The gate creates an inner world.

Maiensäss unterhalb von Soglio, Schweiz – Die Gewichtigkeit des Steins kontrastiert mit der Lebendigkeit des Holzes.

Maiensäss near Soglio, Switzerland – The heaviness of the stone contrasts with the vibrancy of the wood.

Doppelwohnhäuser in Ziefen, Schweiz (Michael Alder, 1970) – Moderner Kontrast zwischen Öffnung und schützendem Steinwerk.

Twin residential houses in Ziefen, Switzerland (Michael Alder, 1970) – Modern contrast between openness and protective masonry.

Felsen auf dem Grimselpass – Der Gletscher schichtet und formt.

Cliff at the Grimsel Pass – The glacier provides layers and shape.

Steinplatte am Lily Pool im Lincoln Park, Chicago (Alfred Caldwell, 1936) – Der Landschaftsgestalter schichtet und formt.

Stone slab at Lily Pool in Lincoln Park, Chicago (Alfred Caldwell, 1936) – The landscape designer adds layers and shape.

Jacobs House in Madison, Wisconsin (Frank Lloyd Wright, 1936–1937) – Der Backstein als Grundmass des Gesamtensembles.

Jacobs House in Madison, Wisconsin (Frank Lloyd Wright, 1936–1937) – The brick as the basic unit of the ensemble.

Farmhouse in Bristol, Wisconsin (Alfred Caldwell, 1948–1985) – Das Mass des Einfachen.

Farmhouse in Bristol, Wisconsin (Alfred Caldwell, 1948–1985) – Utter simplicity.

Mondtore als Zugänge zu den kaiserlichen Hofbauten in Peking – Schwellen zur himmlischen Welt des Herrschers.

Moon gates as entry ways to the imperial residence in Beijing – Threshold to the ruler's divine world.

Friedhof Brion in San Vito d'Altivole, Treviso, Italien (Carlo Scarpa, 1970–1975) – Der Ort, wo sich der diesseitige und der jenseitige Kreis überschneiden.

Brion Cemetery in San Vito d'Altivole, Treviso, Italy (Carlo Scarpa, 1970–1975) – The place where where the earthly and otherworldly circles overlap.

4 KONSTRUKTION
CONSTRUCTION

Last und Stütze – Primat der Säule, Entfaltung der Struktur
Elemente des modernen Bauens

Burden of the pillar – primal column, emergence of the structure
Elements of modern construction

Tempel der Athene auf Aigina, Griechenland (5. Jahrhundert v. Chr.) / Nationalgalerie in Berlin von Mies van der Rohe (1962–1968) (Collage des Autors).

Temple of Athena on Aegina Island, Greece (5th century BCE) – Nationalgalerie in Berlin by Mies van der Rohe (1962–1968) (collage by the author).

Trias-Element, Bausystem (Werner Blaser, 1972–1974) – Bauen mit dem Baukastenprinzip in Containernorm, klare Gliederung von Tragwerk und Ausfüllung im Skelett.

Triadic element, construction system (Werner Blaser, 1972–1974) – Construction with the modular building concept according to the dimensions of containers. Clear division of support structure and design in the fram

Stahlstützen, IIT Alumni Memorial Hall, Chicago (Mies van der Rohe, 1945) – Das konstruktive Prinzip ist ablesbar.

Steel supports, IIT Alumni Memorial Hall, Chicago (Mies van der Rohe, 1945) – The structural principle is clearly communicated.

4 CONSTRUCTION Elements of modern construction

Stahlstützen am Kirchgemeindezentrum Neuenburg, Deutschland (Werner Blaser, 1967) – Die Gestaltgebung entsteht aus der Konstruktion.

Steel supports on the parish center in Neuenburg, Germany (Werner Blaser, 1967) – The design is derived from the construction.

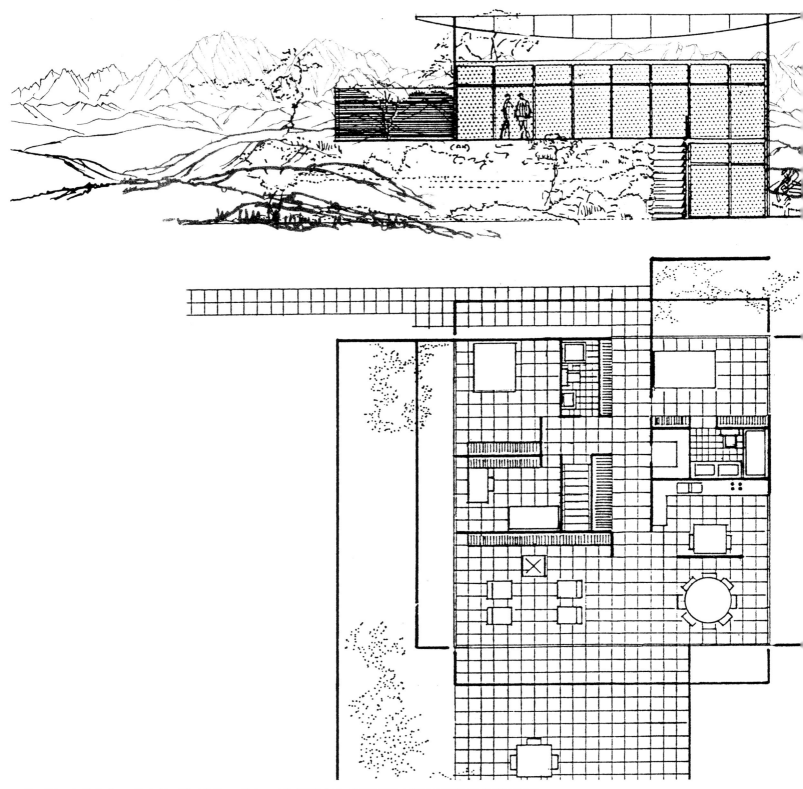

Haus Geisendorf in Esslingen, Deutschland (Projekt Werner Blaser, 1992) – Das Dach als universale Lösung für die verschiedensten Funktionen.

Haus Geisendorf in Esslingen, Germany (project by Werner Blaser, 1992) – The roof serves as a universal solution that serves a great variety of purposes.

Terrasse in Kishi mit Ausblick auf den Onegasee, Karelien, Russland (14.–19. Jahrhundert) – Die Konstruktion gibt den Blick in die Weite frei.

Terrace in Kishi with a view of Lake Onega, Karelia, Russia (14th to 19th century) – The construction opens up onto an expansive view.

Nationalgalerie Berlin (Mies van der Rohe, 1962–1968) – Die nach aussen gesetzte Konstruktion erweitert den Innenraum.

Nationalgalerie Berlin (Mies van der Rohe, 1962–1968) – By shifting the construction outwards the interior space is extended.

Innenraum der klassischen kaiserlichen Shugaku-in Villa in Kyoto (1629) – Bedingt durch das Tragskelett wird der leere Raum zum Gefäss der Fülle.

Interior hall of the classical Shugaku-in Imperial Villa in Kyoto (1629) – The supporting frame turns the open space into a container of abundance.

Farnsworth House in Plano, Illinois (Mies van der Rohe, 1945–1950) – Eine Architektur der Leere.

Farnsworth House in Plano, Illinois (Mies van der Rohe, 1945–1950) – An architecture of emptiness.

Haus Garkov mit kanneliertem Säulenschaft aus Holz in Koprivstiza, Bulgarien (19. Jahrhundert) – Bewährtes aus klassizistischen Gestaltungsformen.

Garkov House with fluted wooden columns in Koprivstiza, Bulgaria (19th century) – Proven construction derived from classical design forms.

Kreuzgewölbe mit sechs feingliedrigen Eisenstützen, Hauptpost Basel (Johann Jakob Stehlin, 1878–1880) – Neues orientiert sich am Bewährten.

Cross vault with six delicate iron supports, main post office in Basel (Johann Jakob Stehlin, 1878–1880) – New designs based on proven construction techniques.

Japanischer Schirm aus Bambus – Der geöffnete Schirm als Parallele zum Fachwerk.

Japanese bamboo umbrella – The opened umbrella offers a parallel to half-timbered constructions.

Renault Centre in Swindon, Grossbritannien (Norman Foster, 1980–1983) – Spielerischer Umgang mit einer technischen Entwicklung.

Renault Centre in Swindon, UK (Norman Foster, 1980–1983) – Playful approach to technical development.

Hôtel Tassel in Brüssel (Victor Horta, 1892–1893) – Organische Struktur als Konstruktionselement.

Hôtel Tassel in Brussels (Victor Horta, 1892–1893) – Organic structure as building element.

Renault Centre in Swindon – Nur mit klarer Gestalt und technischer Intelligenz entsteht ein solides Raumgefüge.

Renault Centre in Swindon – Only with clear design and technical intelligence can a solid room structure be created.

Maison Carrée und Carrée d'Art in Nîmes, Frankreich (Norman Foster, 1984–1993) – Respekt gegenüber der Vergangenheit.

Maison Carrée and Carrée d'Art in Nîmes, France (Norman Foster, 1984–1993) – Respect for the past.

Bibliothèque Nationale in Paris (Henri Labrouste, 1857–1867) – Modulare Koordination von Stütze und Lichtführung.

Bibliothèque Nationale in Paris (Henri Labrouste, 1857–1867) – Modular coordination of column and lighting.

United Airlines Terminal, O'Hare Airport Chicago (Helmut Jahn, 1986–1987) – Stahl und Glas als Lichtträger.

United Airlines terminal, O'Hare Airport, Chicago (Helmut Jahn, 1986–1987) – Steel and glass as light elements.

Mercado-Halle in Barcelona – Bei der Entwicklung des Filigran stand die Tradition des Holzgefüges Pate.

Mercado hall in Barcelona – The tradition of woodwork was used in the development of the filigree.

Paraplegikerzentrum Nottwil, Schweiz (Katharina und Wilfrid Steib, 1985–1990) – Mehr Transparenz und Licht durch die Stahlkonstruktion.

Nottwil Center for Paraplegics, Switzerland (Katharina and Wilfrid Steib, 1985–1990) – More transparency and light thanks to the steel construction.

Eiffelturm, Paris (Gustave Eiffel, 1884–1889) – Der dreihundert Meter hohe Turm ist ein Denkmal der Eisenbaukunst.

Eiffel Tower, Paris (Gustave Eiffel, 1884–1889) – The 300-meter high tower is a monument to the art of iron construction.

Eiffelturm – Eisenfachwerk verbindet und hält offen. Das Alte bleibt für das Neue gültig.

Eiffel Tower – The iron frame holds the various elements together while keeping the structure open. The old is integrated into the new.

5 URBILD UND ABBILD
ARCHETYPE AND IMAGE

Urbilder bestimmen das Kreative, vermitteln spontane Einsicht, sensibilisieren die Sinne, ermöglichen das Unterscheidenkönnen von Wert und Unwert

Archetypes define the creative, communicate spontaneous vision, hone the senses, make it possible to distinguish between the valid and invalid

Galleria Vittorio Emanuele II in Mailand (1865) / Gallery in Denver, Colorado (um 1980) (Collage des Autors).
Galleria Vittorio Emanuele II in Milan (1865) / Gallery in Denver, Colorado (ca. 1980) (collage by the author).

Baumgruppe in der Champagne, Frankreich – Transparenz unter dem Blätterdach.

Group of trees in Champagne, France – Lucency under the canopy of leaves.

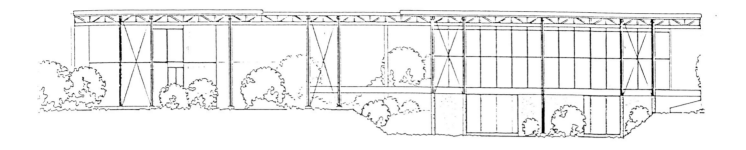

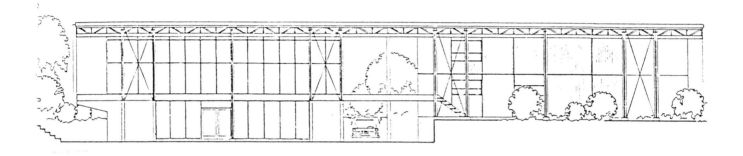

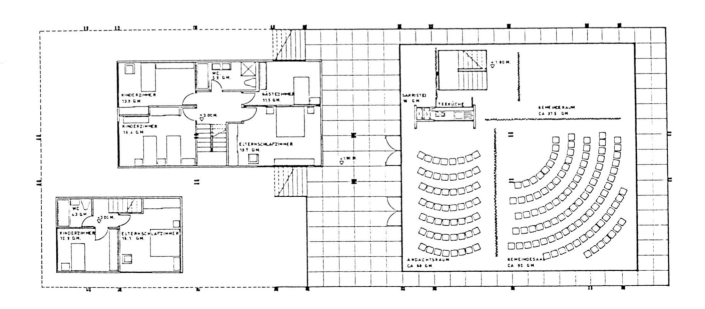

Kirchgemeindehaus Heitersheim, Deutschland (Werner Blaser, 1972) – Transparenz unter Dach und Fach.

Heitersheim parish center, Germany (Werner Blaser, 1972) – Lucency within the house.

Holzhängebrücke im Naturreservat Brule-River, Wisconsin, USA – Rhythmisches Spiel der Holzelemente.

Wooden suspension bridge in a nature reserve, Brule, **Wisconsin** – Rhythmic interplay of wooden elements.

Kletterlabyrinth in Basel (Werner Blaser, 1960) – Moduliertes rhythmisches Spiel.

Recreational labyrinth in Basel (Werner Blaser, 1960) – Modulated rhythmic interplay.

Kragkuppel im Puschlav, Schweiz – Die bienenkorbähnliche Zelle dient als Milchkeller. Das Bauwerk ist Inbegriff einer rundherum gleich gestalteten Einheit.

Cantilevered dome in Puschlav, Switzerland – This hive-like cell is used to store milk. The structure is the perfect example of a uniformly designed single unit.

Lagerhalle mit Büros, Fa. Lüber, Märkt, Deutschland (Werner Blaser, 1970–1971) – Einheitliches Raumfachwerk umschliesst das Dach und alle Seiten.

Warehouse with offices, Lüber company, Märkt, Germany (Werner Blaser, 1970–1971) – Uniform space frame encloses the roof and all sides of the structure.

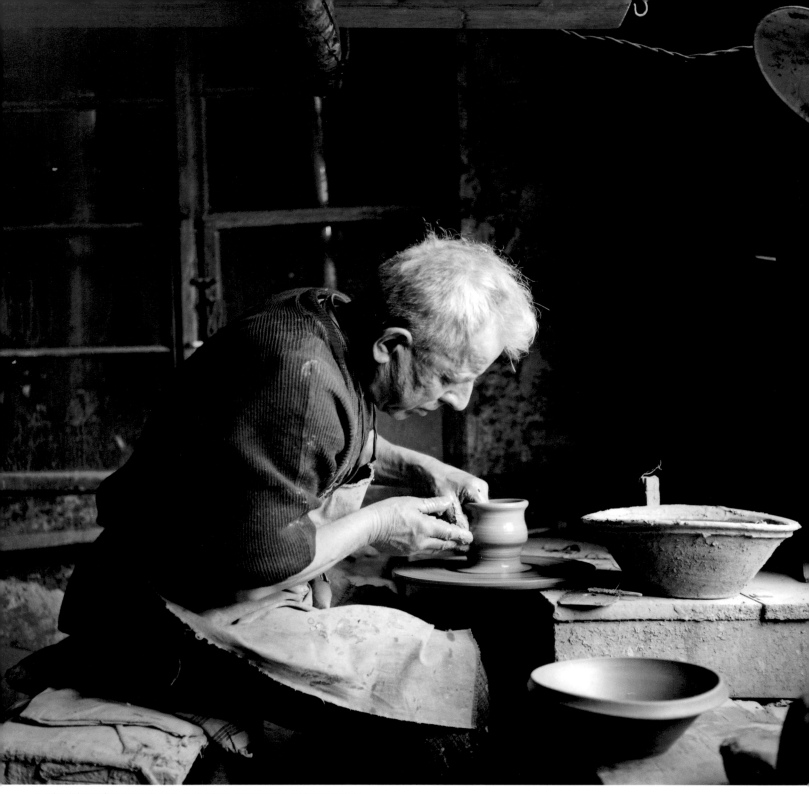

Handwerk des Töpfers Blum in Kandern, Deutschland – Konzentration auf das Wesentliche.

Potter Blum's handwork, Kandern, Germany – Concentrating on the essential.

Chinesischer Hofgarten, Hangchow – Im Sehen Gelassenheit erfahren, um sie im Dasein zu finden.

Chinese courtyard garden, Hangzhou – Experiencing serenity in seeing in order to find serenity in being.

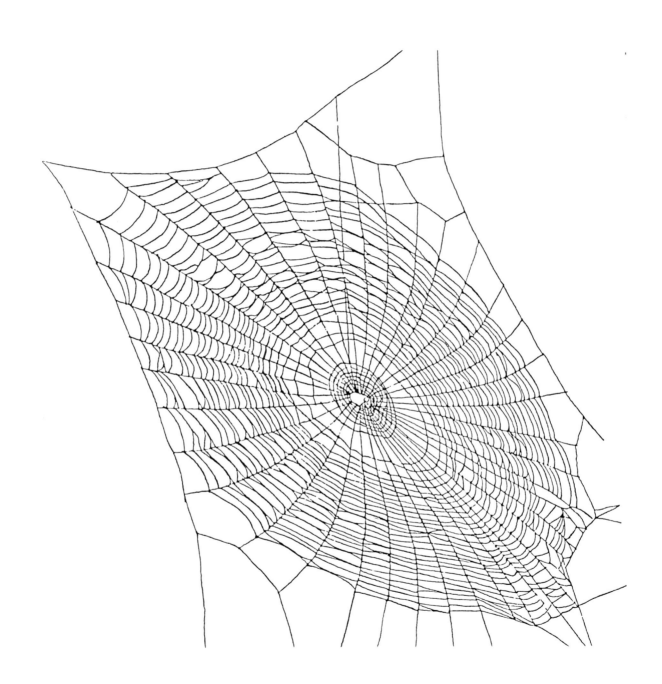

Zeichnung eines Spinnengewebes – Schönheit und Funktionalität in der Natur.

Drawing of a spider web – Beauty and functionality in nature.

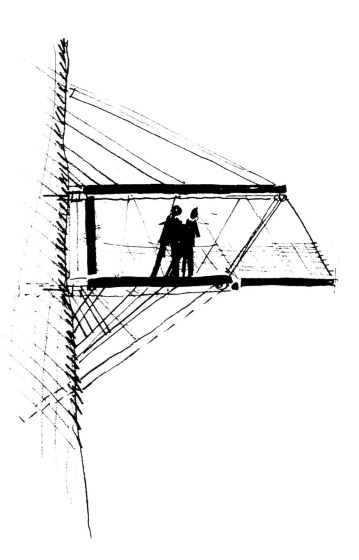

Skizze einer Baumhütte (Norman Foster) – Filigranes Spielen in und mit der Natur.

Sketch of a tree house (Norman Foster) – Filigree interplay in and with nature.

Fachwerkhaus in der Champagne, Frankreich – Zusammenspiel von Gefüge und Füllung.

Half-timbered house in Champagne, France – Interplay of frame and filling.

Charles und Ray Eames House in Pasadena, Kalifornien (1947–1949) – Gefüge und Füllwerk in heutiger Variation.

Charles and Ray Eames House in Pasadena, California (1947–1949) – Modern variation of frame and filling.

Haus Gugalun bei Versam, Schweiz (Peter Zumthor, 1990–1993) – Einbindung des Baus in die Umgebung. An den linken, bestehenden Gebäudeteil wurde der neue rechts angebaut.

Gugalun House near Versam, Switzerland (Peter Zumthor, 1990–1993) – Integration of the structure into the surroundings. The new section of the building to the right was built onto the left, pre-existing section.

Haus Gugalun – Mit waagrecht aufeinandergeschichteten Hölzern wird der alte Blockbau erneuert und zugleich erhalten.

Gugalun House – With wood pieces layered perpendicularly one upon the other the old block construction was renovated and at the same time preserved.

Walsersiedlung in Alagna Valsesia, Italien – Die Hülle dient auf drei Seiten als Terrasse.

Walser colony in Alagna Valsesia, Italy – On three sides the shell serves as a terrace.

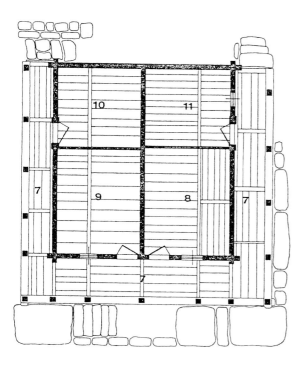

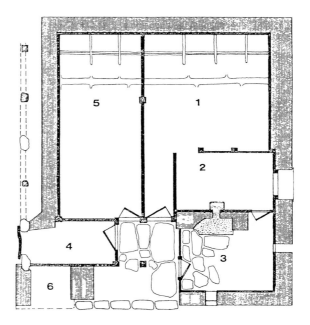

Walsersiedlung – Grundriss und Ansichten.

Walser colony – Blueprint and views.

La Ville d'Hiver in Arcachon, Frankreich – Gleichzeitigkeit der Formgebung um die Jahrhundertwende auf beiden Seiten des Atlantiks.

La Ville d'Hiver in Arcachon, France – Similarities of design on both sides of the Atlantic around the turn of the century.

Stadthäuser in Galveston, Texas – Amerikanische Parallele.

City houses in Galveston, Texas – American parallels.

Galleria Vittorio Emanuele II in Mailand (Giuseppe Mengoni, 1865) – Die Decke als lichtdurchlässiger Schirm.

Galleria Vittorio Emanuele II in Milan (Giuseppe Mengoni, 1865) – The roof as translucent screen.

Gallery in Denver, Colorado – Der transparente Schirm schafft eine multifunktionale Raumnutzung.

Gallery in Denver, Colorado – The transparent screen creates a multi-functional interior space.

Fischerkörbe aus Hongkong; Geflecht aus gespaltenem Bambus – Die Öffnungen variieren geometrische Grundfiguren.

Fishing baskets from Hong Kong, wickerwork from cleaved bamboo – Openings in the shape of various basic geometrical forms.

Haus Melnikow in Moskau (Konstantin Melnikow, 1927) – Im Rund der Wände spielen die Licht- und Fensteröffnungen mit geradlinigen, geometrischen Formen.

Melnikov House in Moscow (Konstantin Melnikov, 1927) – The light and window openings feature linear, geometrical forms in the circularity of the walls.

Japanischer Wasserschöpfer – Traditionelles Gerät für die Teezeremonie aus Bambus. Kostbarkeit von allereinfachster Gestalt mit formvollendetem Griff (Morgenland).

Japanese water ladle – Traditional tool for the tea ceremony made from bamboo. Treasure of the simplest of all forms with perfectly shaped handle (Eastern World).

Spezialhammer – Vollendung im Detail und in der Handhabung auch im Abendland.

Eastern world – Treasure of the simplest of all forms with perfectly shaped handle: a special hammer.

6 STILLE
SILENCE

Architektur der Stille, der Leere, der Meditation.
Einfachheit und Natürlichkeit als Ethik der Architektur

Architecture of silence, emptiness, meditation. Simplicity
and naturalness as the ethics of architecture

Plattform von Tadao Ando auf der Insel Naoshima (1988–1995) / Traditionelle japanische Schiebetür aus Reispapier (Collage des Autors).

Tadao Ando platform on Naoshima Island (1988–1995) / Traditional Japanese sliding door made of rice paper (collage by the author).

Casa Nascosta in Ascona, Schweiz (Werner Blaser, 1977) – Erweiterung eines lokalen Steinhauses durch eine Pergola.

Casa Nascosta in Ascona, Switzerland (Werner Blaser, 1977) – Extension of a local stone house by means of a pergola.

Casa Nascosta – Im Gegensatz zum undurchlässigen Stein, der den bergenden Innenraum schafft, bezieht das transparente Balkenwerk des Holzes die natürliche Umgebung mit ein.

Casa Nascosta – In stark contrast to the impervious stone, which structures the containing interior space, the transparent woodwork integrates the natural surroundings.

Cor-ten-Stahlskeletthaus im Rohbau in Bottmingen, Schweiz (Werner Blaser 1968–1969) – Öffnung nach aussen, Konzentration nach innen in bescheidener Backstein-Stahlkonstruktion.

Cor-ten steel frame building frame in Bottmingen, Switzerland (Werner Blaser 1968–1969). Opening outwards, concentration inwards with modest brick-steel construction.

Stahlskeletthaus in Bottmingen – Die Konstruktion bleibt im Eingangsbereich sichtbar.

Steel frame house in Bottmingen – The framework remains visible in the entrance area.

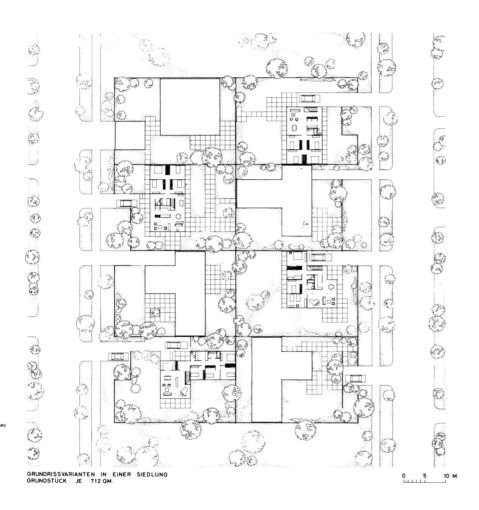

SCHNITT DURCH HOF

ANSICHT VON STRASSE

HOFHÄUSER AUS EINEM BAUKASTENSYSTEM

VARIABLES STAHLSKELETT (TRAGKONSTRUKTION 3.60 / 3.60 M.) MIT DEMONTIER -
BAREN UND FLEXIBLEN WANDELEMENTEN (GRUNDRISSMODUL 1.20 M.)

ARCHITEKTEN: WERNER BLASER   SWB / BDA   BASEL
MITARBEITER: HUGO IMHOLZ, ERNEST PERSCHE

NORD

GRUNDRISSVARIANTEN IN EINER SIEDLUNG
GRUNDSTÜCK JE 712 QM.

0   5   10 M.

Hofhausprojekt, Grundmodul 1,20 m (Werner Blaser, 1971–1972) – Gegen die Zersiedelung: die Idee der horizontalen Stadt. Leben mit der Natur im umschlossenen Raum, wo aussen und innen eins sind.

Courtyard house project, basic module 1.20 m (Werner Blaser, 1971–1972) – Combating sprawl: the idea of the horizontal city. Life with nature in an enclosed space where exterior and interior become one.

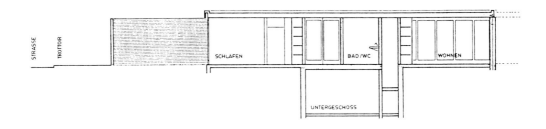

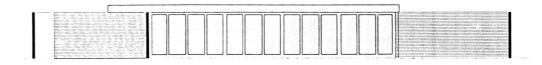

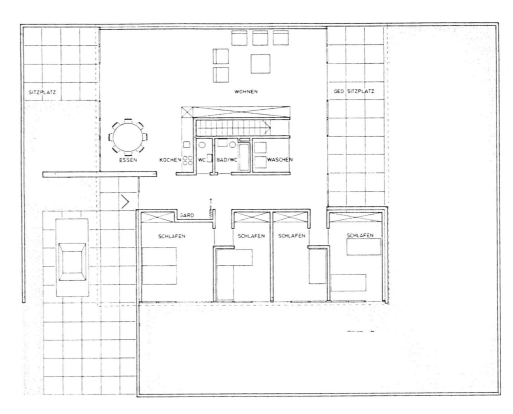

Hofhausprojekt – Der nach aussen abgegrenzte Garten macht die Natur zu einem Stück Innenraum.

Courtyard house project – The garden is separated from the outside turning nature into a kind of interior space.

860 Lake Shore Drive Apartments in Chicago (Mies van der Rohe, 1948–1951) – Die Landschaft ist Bestandteil der Architektur.

860 Lake Shore Drive apartments in Chicago (Mies van der Rohe, 1948–1951) – The landscape is part of the architecture.

Jun Port Island Building in Kobe, Japan (Tadao Ando, 1983–1985) – Der stille Raum macht Sehen und Erleben zum Wesentlichen.

Jun Port Island Building in Kobe, Japan (Tadao Ando, 1983–1985) – In the silent space vision and experience become essential elements.

Vitra Konferenzpavillon in Weil am Rhein, Deutschland (Tadao Ando, 1991–1993) – Das Gebäude versinkt in der Natur: Kirschbäume bestimmen die Gebäudehöhe.

Vitra conference pavilion in Weil am Rhein, Germany (Tadao Ando, 1991–1993) – The building recedes into the surrounding nature: cherry trees determine the height of the building.

Vitra Konferenzpavillon – Verkörperung der Stille im abgesenkten Geschoss.

Vitra conference pavilion – Embodiment of silence in the story built into the ground.

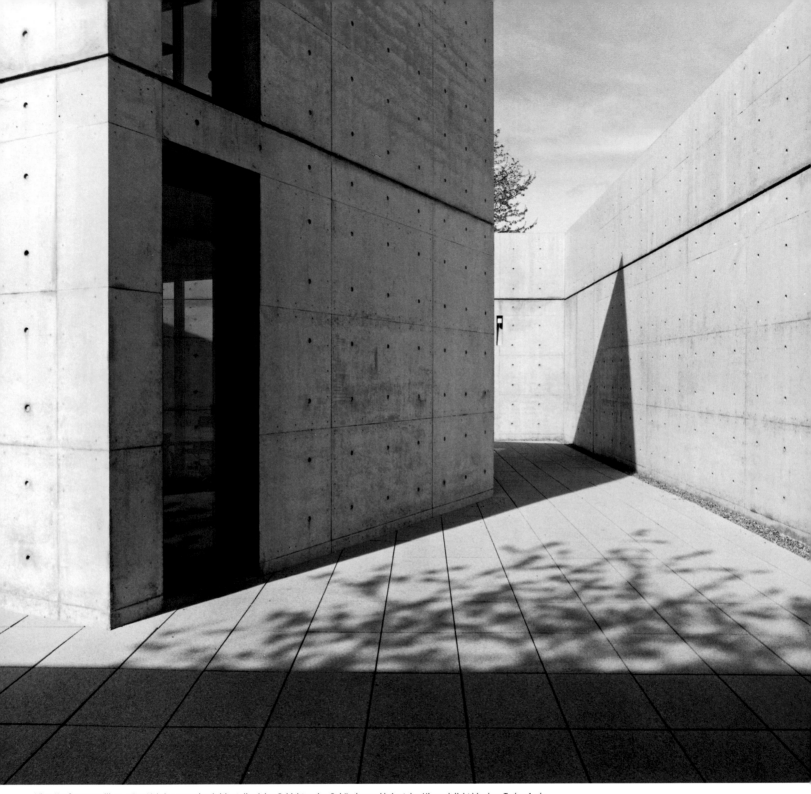

Vitra Konferenzpavillon – «Der Lichtbrunnen durchdringt die vielen Schichten des Gebäudes und bringt das Himmelslicht hinein.» *Tadao Ando*

Vitra conference pavilion – "The light fountain permeates the various layers of the building and allows the light from the sky to enter." *Tadao Ando*

Vitra Konferenzpavillon – Die Schlichtheit des Gebäudes und seine Vertiefung ins Erdreich lassen die Schönheit der Natur hervortreten.

Vitra conference pavilion – The plainness of the building and its immersion in the earth allow the beauty of nature to come to the fore.

Des Moines Art Center, Iowa (Eliel Saarinen, 1948; Anbauten: Ieoh Ming Pei 1965, Richard Meier 1985) – Drei Architektengenerationen gaben dem Museumsbau seine jetzige Gestalt.

Des Moines Art Center, Iowa (Eliel Saarinen, 1948; extensions: Ieoh Ming Pei 1965, Richard Meier 1985) – Three generations of architects gave the museum structure its current form.

Des Moines Art Center – Jede Generation trug ihren Teil bei, bis hin zum Bauwerk ganz in Weiss mit kompakten Materialmassen, die sich in Leichtigkeit auflösen.

Des Moines Art Center – Every generation made a unique contribution, culminating in the white structure with compact material masses that dissolve into lightness.

Primarschule ai Saleggi in Locarno, Schweiz (Livio Vacchini, 1972–1979) – Rhythmischer Wohlklang durch Massteilung, Transparenz und Massen.

Ai Saleggi primary school in Locarno, Switzerland (Livio Vacchini, 1972–1979) – Rhythmic euphony created by means of division of mass, transparence and ideal dimensions.

Primarschule in Locarno – Spielerische Leichtigkeit.

Primary school in Locarno – Playful lightness.

Villa Reinhardt in Winterthur, Schweiz (Rittmeyer & Furrer, 1928) – Gartendetail, das zu Stille und Meditation einlädt.

Villa Reinhardt in Winterthur, Switzerland (Rittmeyer & Furrer, 1928) – Garden detail that inspires silence and meditation.

Zweidimensionales Gitterwerk bei der Fondation Cartier in Paris – Weckt die Illusion räumlicher Tiefe.

Two-dimensional lattice at the Fondation Cartier in Paris – Gives the illusion of spatial depth.

Eingangstor im Geburtshaus von Constantin Brâncuşi in Hobiţa, Rumänien – Impulsgeber für das spätere Kunstwerk *Tor des Kusses*.

Entryway into the birth house of Constantin Brâncuşi in Hobiţa, Romania – Inspiration for the later work *Gate of the Kiss*.

Das *Tor des Kusses* in Tirgu Jui, Rumänien (Skulptur Constantin Brâncuşi, 1937) – Der Impuls ist zum Kunstwerk geworden, das den Hindurchschreitenden nicht unverwandelt lässt.

Gate of the Kiss in Târgu Jui, Romania (sculpture by Constantin Brâncuşi, 1937) – The original inspiration has become a work of art that leaves no one who passes through untransformed.

Fatehpur Sikri, eine kaiserliche Residenz bei Agra, Rajasthan (1569) – Filigrane, in Stein gehauene Gitterwand.

Fatehpur Sikri, an imperial residence near Agra, Rajasthan (1569) – Filigree lattice wall carved in stone.

Fatehpur Sikri, Mausoleum Salim Chisti (1572 n. Chr.) – Bei aller Grösse der Gesamtanlage bewahrt der Plan die Bescheidenheit der Stille und vermeidet die Überfüllung des Raumes.

Fatehpur Sikri, Salim Chisti Mausoleum (1572 CE) – Despite the enormous size of the overall facility the plan conveys the humility of the silence and manages to avoid overfilling the space.

Taos Pueblo in Taos, New Mexico – In ihrer Einfachheit, Zweckmässigkeit und Geschlossenheit edle Lehmarchitektur.

Taos Pueblo in Taos, New Mexico – Adobe architecture that is noble in its simplicity, purposefulness and coherence.

Palast im Pichola-See in Udaipur, Rajasthan – Als Ort des Rückzugs und der Meditation mitten im See errichtet.

Palace on Pichola Lake in Udaipur, Rajasthan – Erected as a place for withdrawal and meditation in the middle of the lake.

Rede beim Fest der Freunde zum 70. Geburtstag von Werner Blaser, 21. August 1994

Lieber Werner, liebe Geburtstagsfestversammlung,
meine Damen und Herren,

ich bin kein Redner. Wenn ich heute dennoch reden soll, so liegt das an Christian, unserem Festorganisator, und an der Vermutung, dass die Zahl der Jahresringe am Baum der Freundschaft zwischen dir, Werner, und mir – im Vergleich zu den anderen derartigen Bäumen – mit 47 wohl am Grössten ist. Und bei einem Fest der Freunde kommt der quasi dienstälteste Freund nicht um den Versuch herum, etwas vom Sinn dieses Festes zur Sprache zu bringen.
Wovon soll ich nun aber reden, wenn der Jubilar seinen 70. Geburtstag lediglich als Anlass zu diesem Fest sehen will, und das Fest selbst nicht ihm, sondern seinen Freunden zugeeignet sein soll?

Lieber Werner, ich habe verstanden, dass du nicht dich, sondern deinen Freundeskreis im Mittelpunkt dieses Festes sehen willst. Man könnte versucht sein, diese deine Haltung mit Bescheidenheit in Verbindung zu bringen. Entspringt sie aber nicht vielmehr einer Ahnung, einem verborgenen Wissen um das Wesen des Festes? Und zum Wesen des Festes gehört, dass es wegweist von allem Ichbezogenen, Ichhaften hin auf die Festgemeinschaft, die sich bildet, wenn wir gemeinsam bei jenen unsichtbaren Mächten zu Gast sind, die auch das Fest mit seiner Fülle stiften.
Dennoch kommen wir nicht darum herum, die logische Konsequenz zu ziehen, dass dieser Freundeskreis – wie jeder Kreis – einen Mittelpunkt hat. Und der Mittelpunkt, um den herum sich unser Kreis hier konstituiert, heisst nun einmal Werner Blaser. Deshalb ist es unausweichlich, lieber Werner, hier und heute auch von dir zu reden.
Am Fest der Freunde geht es aber nicht um den Werner Blaser an und für sich, sondern um den Werner Blaser für und mit uns; also um die Freundschaft, die jeden von uns mit ihm verbindet. Und dazu hätte wohl jeder Anwesende etwas zu sagen. Im kleineren Kreis könnte jeder das Seine zu dieser Freundschaftsrede beitragen. Hier im grösseren Kreis kann einer zwar nicht für alle reden, aber er kann wenigstens versuchen, aus subjektiver Sicht das aufleuchten zu lassen, was die Freundschaft mit Werner Blaser bestimmt.
Hölderlin hat einmal die Zeit seit dem Beginn einer Freundschaft markiert mit den Worten «[...] seit ein Gespräch wir sind [...]». In diesem «Zusammen-ein-Gespräch-Sein» lässt sich erkennen, was Freundschaft bedeutet. Zum Gespräch gehört auf beiden Seiten beides: Das *Zuhören-Können* und das *Etwas-zu-sagen-Haben*, oder mit anderen Worten: Offenheit und Eigenheit. Wir wären nicht mit Werner befreundet, wenn *er* uns nichts zu sagen hätte, und wenn *wir* nicht offen wären für das, was er *uns* zu sagen hat. Entsprechend gilt das Umgekehrte.
Was ist das, was er uns zu sagen hat? Oder, nach dem Gleichen anders gefragt: Was sind seine Eigenheiten?

Speech held on the occasion of Werner Blaser's 70th birthday on 29 August 1994

Dear Werner and Guests of This Birthday Celebration:

I am no public speaker. If I am nevertheless to deliver a speech today it is because of Christian, the organizer of this celebration, and because the number of rings on the tree of friendship between you, Werner, and me – 47 – is would appear to be greater than that of any of the other trees present. For at a celebration of friends it is the longest serving friend's duty to attempt to express in words the meaning of the gathering.

Yet what should I speak about when the man whose 70th birthday it is considers the event little more than an excuse to organize a celebration not for him, but for his friends?

Dear Werner, I understand that you would like your friends and not yourself to stand at the center of this gathering. One might be tempted to attribute this attitude to modesty, but doesn't it have far more to do with a notion, a kind of secret knowledge, of the nature of celebration itself? Part of this nature is a disavowal of egotistical, selfish considerations in favor of the celebratory community that comes together when we become guests of the invisible powers that enrich such gatherings.

And yet we cannot avoid the logical conclusion that this circle of friends – like every circle – has a center point. And the center around which our circle turns bears the name of Werner Blaser. For this reason it is inevitable, dear Werner, that you will be spoken of on this occasion.

At this celebration of friends we are not, however, concerned with Werner Blaser in isolation, but with the Werner Blaser with and among us, and the friendship that connects each of us to him. Everyone present today could surely say a few words about this friendship, and at a smaller gathering this would be possible. And while at this larger gathering one person cannot speak for everyone, one person can at least attempt to bring to light from a subjective point of view that which has formed the basis of our friendship with Werner Blaser.

Hölderlin once referred to the beginning of a friendship with the words "... since we are a conversation ...". In this "being a conversation together" we can learn what friendship really means. Essential to any conversation is that both sides offer both elements: *being able to listen* and *having something to say*. Or in other words: openness and uniqueness. We would not be friends of Werner if *he* had nothing to say to us and if *we* were not open to that which he has to say to *us*. The reverse is also true.

And what does he have to say to us? Or – to put it in the terms suggested above – what are his unique qualities?

Als wir uns vor 47 Jahren kennenlernten, waren wir beide begeistert engagiert in einer Bewegung, die glaubte, die Welt dadurch erneuern zu können, dass sie dem Einzelnen die Dimension eines weltweiten Miteinanders nach christlichen Massstäben eröffnete. Wenn junge Menschen, von Idealen begeistert, ihre jugendliche Identität in einer kollektiven Bewegung finden, werden die individuellen Eigenheiten in der Gruppe eher nivelliert als gestärkt. So war es damals auch bei uns. Wir kamen einander vertraut vor, ohne uns eigentlich begegnet zu sein. Die Identifizierung mit den Gruppenzielen verzögerte das Differenzieren und Kultivieren des Individuellen. Eine Postkarte mit der Abbildung eines Werkes von Paul Klee, die Werner mir geschickt hatte, wurde zum Anlass dafür, dass das eigentliche Gespräch zwischen uns in Gang kam.

Es war nicht einfach nur das gemeinsame Interesse für moderne Kunst, das uns damals miteinander verband. Beide spürten wir zu jener Zeit, wie notwendig für unsere damalige Welt ein Bilden, Bauen, Aufbauen, Gestalten, ein kulturelles Schaffen war, das dem Geist und der Sensibilität entsprach, wie sie uns in jenen künstlerisch so wertvollen Aussagen begegnete, die zuvor von der kollektiven Dummheit als «entartete Kunst» diffamiert worden war.

Martin Heidegger musste uns, obwohl das schon den Brüdern Grimm bekannt war, wieder ins Bewusstsein rufen, dass unser Wort «bauen» aus dem Altgermanischen *beon* abgeleitet ist, das «bleiben», «wohnen», «sein» bedeutet und in unserem «ich bin» noch lebendig ist. Wir müssten also eigentlich wissen, dass die Frage nach dem «rechten Bauen» an die Frage rührt, wer und wie ich bin.

Ich denke, das ist etwas von dem, was Werner Blaser uns zu sagen hat. Nur sagt er es nicht in Worten. Es ist nicht seine Art, über die Sache, auf die er hinweisen will, zu sprechen. Es ist ein Stück seiner Eigenheit, hinter die Sache zurückzutreten und sie selbst sprechen zu lassen; so etwa, wenn er uns gute Architektur bild- und beispielhaft vor Augen führen will. Er will lieber etwas den Augen zu zeigen als den Ohren zu sagen haben. Und obwohl er ein Wissen davon hat, dass die Frage nach dem rechten Bauen an die Frage rührt: Wer und wie bin ich?, redet er doch kaum davon. Er will keine Moral predigen. Für sich selbst setzt er es aber als selbstverständlich voraus, dass vom künstlerisch Wohlgeordneten aussen ein Anspruch nach innen wirkt und umgekehrt. Deshalb führte ihn diese Frage nach dem rechten Bauen auch nach Japan, wo er der Welt des Zen begegnete, in der das Wissen davon, dass Harmonie aussen mit Harmonie innen korrespondiert, wohl noch am lebendigsten ist. Er kam, wie wir wissen, von Mies van der Rohe dorthin, der sein architektonisches Wollen gern mit dem Augustin-Wort begründete, Schönheit sei das Strahlen der Wahrheit.

In jener Wahrheit, die sich in der altjapanischen Architektur und überhaupt in der Kunst des Zen offenbarte, fand Werner Blaser sich auf seinem eigenen Weg bestätigt. Die Welt des Zen vermittelte ihm ausserdem

When we met 47 years ago Werner and I were both enthusiastically engaged in a movement that we believed could rejuvenate the world, revealing to individuals the possibilities of a global community in accordance with Christian values. When young people who are inspired by ideals find their young identity in a collective movement, individual qualities within the group tend to be muted, not accentuated. That was the case for us as well. We seemed to know each other well, though we had never really encountered one another. The identification with the goals of the group slowed down the process by which distinctions are drawn between people and the individual comes to the fore. A postcard with the image of a work by Paul Klee that Werner sent to me was the occasion upon which the actual conversation between us began in earnest.

It wasn't just our common interest in modern art that connected us back then. At the time we both felt how necessary creation, construction, development and formation were for our world – cultural activities with the spirit and sensibility we found in the valuable artistic statements once vilified by collective stupidity as "degenerate art".

Though the Brothers Grimm already knew it, it was Martin Heidegger who reminded us that our German word *bauen* (to build) is derived from the old German *beon*, which meant to "remain", "inhabit" or "be", and that lives on in the phrase *ich bin* (I am). Therefore we should know that the question as to "correct construction" is very closely related to the question as to who and what I am.

I think that this is part of what Werner Blaser has to say to us. Except that he doesn't say it in words. It's not his way to express the things he finds important with language. It is part of his uniqueness that he is able to withdraw behind objects and to let them speak for themselves – such as when he wishes to show us images and examples of good architecture. He would rather reveal truths to the eyes than say them to the ears. And though he knows that the question as to what constitutes correct construction is related to the question of who and what I am, he hardly ever speaks of this. He does not want to preach. However, he considers it self-evident that external artistic arrangements challenge us internally and the other way around. For this reason the question as to correct construction led him to Japan, where he encountered the world of Zen, a tradition in which the knowledge that external harmony corresponds to inner harmony seems to be most alive. He came, as we know, to Japan from Mies van der Rohe, who grounded his architectural vision on the sentiment of St. Augustine that beauty is the reflection of truth.

In the truth that reveals itself in ancient Japanese architecture and Zen art in general Werner Blaser found confirmation for the path that he had chosen. The world of Zen also provided him with very unique experiences regarding the interaction of creative quality and inner discipline.

auf ganz besonders differenzierte Weise spezielle Erfahrungen der Wechselwirkung zwischen gestalteter Qualität und innerer Disziplin.

In seinem Buch *Tempel und Teehaus in Japan* hat uns Werner Blaser neben vielem anderen gezeigt, wie es die Gartengestaltung des Zen vermeidet, Wege zielgerichtet anzulegen. Kein Weg führt auf geradem Weg zum Tor oder zu einem sonstigen Übergang in einen anderen Bereich. Denn das käme der Ausrichtung auf ein Ziel gleich. Und auf ein Ziel ausgerichtet kann nur das Ich sein.
Die so entstehende Ruhelosigkeit unterscheidet sich von der stillen Gelassenheit des «wahren Selbst», wie es sonst im Zen erfahren wird. Damit der Schreitende durch das Ziel nicht verführt wird, der Ruhe und Stille seines wahren Selbst zu entgleiten, führen in der Gartengestaltung des Zen die Trittsteine, die den Weg markieren, den auf ihnen Schreitenden erst bei den allerletzten Schritten im abgebogenen Winkel auf den Durchgang zu. Diese Anordnung der Trittsteine fordert zu einem meditativen Gehen auf.

Das Wort «meditativ» ist von der indogermanischen Sprachwurzel *med*- abgeleitet, aus der sich im Deutschen Worte wie «messen», «Mass» oder im Lateinischen Worte wie «meditare», «modus», aber auch «medicus» gebildet haben. Der medicus ist der Heilkundige; er vermag das rechte Mass, die heilende Mass-Nahme zu ermessen. Das rechte Mass hat einen Bezug zur Mitte. Davon ist etwas zu erkennen, wenn wir auf einer Waage, die zwei Waagschalen hat, das Gleichgewicht zwischen den beiden Waagschalen herstellen, um so das rechte Mass abzuwägen. Messen und Abwägen, das Bemühen um das rechte Mass – all das hat etwas Meditatives.

Im Zen aber – und das Wort Zen hat ja selbst die Bedeutung «Meditation» – ist Meditieren keine Tätigkeit, sondern ein Sich-Öffnen. Aber wofür? – Es lässt sich nur im Beispiel sagen: Etwa ein Sich-Öffnen für eine Rose, die blüht. Es geht also darum, sich für eine Erfahrung zu öffnen – in unserem Beispiel um die Erfahrung, die mir nur die blühende Rose zu vermitteln vermag.

Beim Streben nach einem Ziel kann ich die Rose leicht übersehen. Oder das Ziel bestimmt mir, keine Zeit für die Rose zu haben oder zu wenig Zeit, um mich ihr so weit zu öffnen, dass sich mir ihr Wesenskern und in ihm etwas vom wahren Selbst erschliesst.

Der Streber, der nur nach Zielen strebt, versäumt solch meditatives Gehen. Er wird von äusseren Zielen, nicht von der Mitte her bestimmt. Auch der Getriebene, der von der Masslosigkeit des Wünschens und Wollens getrieben ist, kann diesen meditativen Weg nicht beschreiten. Beide können mit dem lebendigen Rhythmus nicht Schritt halten und geraten durch ihre arhythmischen Fehltritte ins Stolpern.

In his book *The Temple and Teahouse in Japan* Werner Blaser shows us, among other insights, how in the design of Zen gardens, paths that lead directly to a destination are avoided. No path leads straight to a gate or any other kind of passageway. This would be akin to striving after a goal, and only the ego strives after goals.

The lack of peace that results from such striving is completely unlike the stillness and serenity of the "true self" that is usually experienced in Zen culture. So that walkers are not moved to lose the peace and stillness of their true selves in the presence of a goal, the stepping stones of Zen gardens only lead to passageways at sharp angles at the very end of a path. This arrangement of stepping stones requires one to walk meditatively.

The word "meditative" itself was derived from the Indo-Germanic root *med*-, from which the German words *messen* (measure), *Mass* (mass) or such Latin words as *meditare*, *modus* and even *medicus* evolved. *medicus* means "physician" – one who provides the correct mass or healing measures. The right mass relates to the center or middle. We experience this when we stand on a scale that has two trays and have to achieve a balance in order to estimate the correct mass. Measuring and estimating – striving for the right measure – all these things have something meditative about them.

In Zen – the word Zen itself means "meditation" – meditation is not an activity but an opening up of oneself. For what purpose? This can only be shown through examples: the way one opens oneself to a blossoming rose. It is about opening oneself to experiences – in our case the experience that only the blossoming rose can communicate.

In striving for a goal the rose can easily be overlooked. Or the goal determines that I don't have time for the rose or have too little time to open myself sufficiently that the essence of the rose and thus something of its true self is revealed to me.

The ambitious, those who chase after goals, cannot experience meditative walking. They are guided by external goals, not by their own centers. Nor can those driven by immoderate desire and wanting set forth on this meditative path. They cannot keep pace with the living rhythm – their false, arrhythmic steps cause them to stumble.

Part of the uniqueness of our friend Werner Blaser is that his life has come to manifest something of this meditative step and continues to do so. Never in the course of his long career have any of his colleagues had to fear a desire on his part for power or domination or felt a competitive will in him, as he is not guided by ambitions. The question of meaningful architecture and design has always been more imperative for him than the question as to what

In der Gartenanlage der klassischen kaiserlichen Katsura-Villa in Kyoto (1602 n. Chr.).

In the gardens of the Katsura Imperial Villa in Kyoto (1602 CE).

Zur Eigenheit unseres Freundes Werner Blaser gehört, dass sein Leben etwas von diesem meditativen Gehen verwirklicht hat und noch verwirklicht. Auf seinem langen Berufsweg hatte nie einer seiner Kollegen von ihm ein Macht- oder Dominanzstreben zu befürchten, keiner je seine Konkurrenz, denn er liess sich nicht von ehrgeizigen Zielen bestimmen. Die Frage nach bedeutender Architektur oder bedeutendem Design war ihm stets wesentlicher als die Frage, welche Rolle er selbst dabei spielen könnte. Nicht Abschlüsse und Testate, die ihm seine Karriere erleichtert hätten, interessierten ihn. Fesseln konnte ihn nur ein überzeugendes Antworten auf seine Frage nach dem rechten Bauen. Zum grossen Geld trieb es ihn nicht, noch strebte er danach. Was er verdiente, stellte er immer wieder in den Dienst seines Fragens und, falls nötig, auch in den Dienst des Publizierens beispielhafter Antwort. Wenn er einem grösseren Publikum in den letzten Jahren durch die Basler Architekturvorträge die Begegnung mit bedeutenden Architekten aus aller Welt ermöglichte, und diese dadurch bedeutende Projekte auch bei uns verwirklichen konnten, ist dies ein Beispiel mehr dafür, wie Werner Blaser Anerkennung weniger für sich als vielmehr einfach für gute Architektur sucht.

Das alles gehört zu seiner Eigenheit, die uns anspricht und die es uns leicht macht, mit ihm «ein Gespräch zu bleiben».

Lieber Werner, wir gratulieren uns, dass wir dich haben!

role he himself might play in this field. Distinctions or certificates that would help him in his professional career have never interested him. Only persuasive answers to his question as to the nature of correct construction have moved him. He was never motivated by or tempted to pursue large sums of money. What he earned he always reinvested in the service of his question and, when necessary, in the publication of exemplary answers. If through the architectural lecture series in Basel over the past several years he has been able to bring a larger audience into contact with important architects from all over the world and these architects have in turn been able to realize major projects in our country, this is another example of how Werner Blaser seeks recognition not for himself but above all for good architecture.

All this is part of his uniqueness, a uniqueness that appeals so much to us and makes it easy to "continue our conversation" with him.

Dear Werner, we can only congratulate ourselves that we have you!

Bücher von / Books by Werner Blaser

Tempel und Teehaus in Japan
Urs Graf, Olten 1955
2. Auflage / 2nd edition 1988
Birkhäuser, Basel

Temples et Jardins au Japon
Albert Morancé, Paris 1956

Japanese Temples and Tea-Houses
F. W. Dodge Corporation, New York 1957

Wohnen und Bauen in Japan /
Classical Dwelling Houses in Japan
Niggli, Niederteufen 1958
2. Auflage/2nd edition
Niggli, Sulgen 2005

Struktur und Gestalt in Japan
Artemis, Zürich 1963

Structure and Form in Japan
Wittenborn & Co., New York 1963

Mies van der Rohe – Die Kunst der
Struktur / L'Art de la Structure
Verlag für Architektur, Zürich 1965
6., überarbeitete und erweiterte Aufla-
ge / 6th, revised and enlarged edition
Birkhäuser, Basel 1997

Mies van der Rohe –
The Art of Structure
Praeger, New York 1965
Thames & Hudson, London 1972
2. Auflage/2nd edition 1993
The Whitney Library of Design,
New York 1993

Mies van der Rohe –
El Arte de la Estructura
Carlos Hirsch, Buenos Aires 1965
Gili, Barcelona 1973

Mies van der Rohe –
Die Kunst der Struktur
– japanische Ausgabe /
  Japanese edition
  A. D. A. Edita, Tokio 1976
– italienische Ausgabe /
  Italian edition
  Zanichelli, Bologna 1977
– niederländische Ausgabe /
  Dutch edition
  Uitgeverij, Rotterdam 1986

– portugiesische Ausgabe/
  Portuguese edition
  Martins Fontes, São Paulo 1994

Objektive Architektur –
Beispiel «Skin and Skeleton» /
Objective Architecture –
Example «Skin and Skeleton»
Richard Scherpe, Krefeld 1970

Chinesische Pavillon-Architektur /
Chinese Pavilion Architecture
Niggli, Niederteufen 1974

Strukturale Architektur
aus Osteuropa /
Structural Architecture
of Eastern Europe
Zbinden, Basel 1975

Der Fels ist mein Haus /
Le Rocher est ma Demeure /
The Rock is My Home
Wepf, Basel 1976

Struktur und Textur /
Structure and Texture
Richard Scherpe, Krefeld 1976

Prinzip einer Architektur –
Retrospektive 25 Jahre Werner Blaser
Bündner Kunstmuseum, Chur 1977

Mies van der Rohe –
Lehre und Schule /
Principles and School
Birkhäuser, Basel 1977

Mies van der Rohe –
After Mies, Teaching and Principles
Van Nostrand Reinhold, New York
1977

Mies van der Rohe – Continuing the
Chicago School of Architecture
Birkhäuser, Basel 1981
2., erweiterte Auflage /
2nd, enlarged edition 1981

Holz Haus / Maisons de Bois /
Wood Houses
Wepf, Basel 1980
2., erweiterte Auflage /
2nd, enlarged edition 1985

Filigran Architektur /
Architecture en Filigrane /
Filigree Architecture
Wepf, Basel 1980

Hofhaus in China /
Courtyard House in China
Birkhäuser, Basel 1979
2., erweiterte Auflage /
2nd, enlarged edition 1995

Mies van der Rohe –
Mobili e Interni
Electa, Mailand 1980

Mies van der Rohe –
Furniture and Interiors
Academy Editions, London 1980

Mies van der Rohe –
Meubles et Intérieurs
Electa Moniteur, Paris 1980

Mies van der Rohe –
Möbel und Interieurs
Deutsche Verlags-Anstalt,
Stuttgart 1981

Architecture 70/80 in Switzerland
erschienen auf deutsch, französisch,
italienisch, spanisch, portugiesisch /
published in German, French, Italian,
Spanish, Portuguese
Birkhäuser, Basel 1981
2., erweiterte Auflage /
2nd, enlarged edition 1983

Klappstühle / Folding Chairs
Birkhäuser, Basel 1982

Elementare Bauformen /
Elemental Building Forms
Beton, Düsseldorf 1982

Schweizer Holzbrücken /
Ponts de Bois en Suisse /
Wooden Bridges in Switzerland
Birkhäuser, Basel 1982

Bauernhaus der Schweiz
Birkhäuser, Basel 1983

Drawings of Great Buildings /
Zeichnungen Grosser Bauten
Birkhäuser, Basel 1983

Architecture and Nature –
The Work of Alfred Caldwell /
Architecture et Nature –
L'Œuvre d'Alfred Caldwell /
Architektur und Natur –
Das Werk von Alfred Caldwell
Birkhäuser, Basel 1984

Element – System – Möbel
Deutsche Verlags-Anstalt, Stuttgart 1984

Atrium – Lichthöfe seit fünf
Jahrtausenden /
5000 Years of Open Courtyards
Wepf, Basel 1985

Patios – 5000 Años de Evolución
Gili, Barcelona 1997
2. Auflage / 2nd edition 2004

Architektur im Möbel /
Furniture as Architecture
Waser, Zürich 1985

Mies van der Rohe – Less is More
Waser, Zürich 1986

Fantasie in Holz / Fantasy in Wood
Birkhäuser, Basel 1987

Myron Goldsmith –
Bauten und Konzepte
Buildings and Concepts
Birkhäuser, Basel 1987
Rizzoli, New York 1987

China – Tao in der Architektur
Tao in Architecture
mit/with Chao-Kang Chang
Birkhäuser, Basel 1987

Tao – Architectures de Chine
mit/with Chao-Kang Chang
André Delcourt, Lausanne 1988

Santiago Calatrava – Ingenieur-
Architektur / Engineering Architecture
Birkhäuser, Basel 1988
2., erweiterte Auflage /
2nd, enlarged edition 1990
– spanisch/englische Ausgabe /
  Spanish/English edition
  Gili, Barcelona 1989

Richard Meier
Building for Art / Bauen für die Kunst
Birkhäuser, Basel 1990

Tadao Ando – Sketches/Zeichnungen
Birkhäuser, Basel 1990

Ernst Koller 1900–1990
Kontraste eines Ingenieurs
Krebs, Basel 1990

Norman Foster Sketch Book
Birkhäuser, Basel 1991
2. Auflage / 2nd edition 1993

Helmut Jahn – Airports
Birkhäuser, Basel 1991

Bauen vor der Stadt /
Suburban Building
mit/with Dieter Wronsky
Birkhäuser, Basel 1991

Orient/Occident
Beton, Düsseldorf 1991

Fügen und Verbinden /
Joint and Connection
Birkhäuser, Basel 1992

Chicago Architecture
Holabird & Root 1880–1992
Birkhäuser, Basel 1992

Richard Meier – Detail
Birkhäuser, Basel 1993
2. Auflage/2nd edition 1996

Tomsk – Textur in Holz /
Texture in Wood/Texture en Bois
Birkhäuser, Basel 1993

Livio Vacchini – Transformation
Birkhäuser, Basel 1994

Paris – Zurich
Restaurants Paris Belle Epoque
Waser, Zürich 1995

Light Tech – Richard Horden
Birkhäuser, Basel 1995

Holz Pionier Architektur /
Wood Pioneer Architecture
Waser, Zürich 1996

Metall Pionier Architektur /
Metal Pioneer Architecture
Waser, Zürich 1995

Stein Pionier Architektur /
Stone Pioneer Architecture
Waser, Zürich 1996

Helmut Jahn
Transparency/Transparenz
Birkhäuser, Basel 1996

Mies van der Rohe – West Meets East
Birkhäuser, Basel 1996
2., erweiterte Auflage /
2nd, enlarged edition 2001

Renzo Piano – Fondation Beyeler
erschien auf deutsch, englisch,
italienisch / published in German,
English, Italian
Birkhäuser, Basel 1998
2. Auflage / 2nd edition 2001

Renzo Piano – Building Workshop
Museum Beyeler
Benteli, Bern 1998

Werner Sobek
Ingenieur-Kunst/Art of Engineering
Birkhäuser, Basel 1999

Mies van der Rohe – Farnsworth House
Birkhäuser, Basel 1999

Mies van der Rohe
Lake Shore Drive Apartments
Birkhäuser, Basel 1999

Tadao Ando
Museum der Weltkulturen im Rhein
Vice Versa, Berlin 1999

Mies van der Rohe –
West is East is West
Vice Versa, Berlin 2000

Ernst Koller – Erfinder und
Konstrukteur bis zum 100. Lebensjahr /
Investor and Designer at the Age of
100 Years
Wepf, Basel 2000

Begegnungen –
An Architect meets Architects
Birkhäuser, Basel 2000

Nelly Rudin
innen ist aussen /inside is outside
Offizin, Zürich 2000

Christa de Carouge – habit habitat
erschienen auf deutsch,
französisch, englisch / published in
German, French, English
Lars Müller, Baden 2000

Mies van der Rohe – IIT Crown Hall
Birkhäuser, Basel 2001

Ernst Koller: Leben – Wohnen
Wepf, Basel 2001

Tadao Ando – Architektur der Stille /
Architecture of Silence
Birkhäuser, Basel 2001

Powell /Kleinschmidt
Interior Architecture
Birkhäuser, Basel 2001

Renzo Piano – Centre Kanak
Birkhäuser, Basel 2002

Kurt Brägger – Zoo Basel
Reinhardt, Basel 2002

R 128 by Werner Sobek
Bauen im 21. Jahrhundert /
Architecture in the 21st Century
Birkhäuser, Basel 2002

Natur im Gebauten /Nature in Building
Rudolf Steiner in Dornach
Birkhäuser, Basel 2002

Klaus Schuldt /Andreas Scheiwiller
Ensemble Habitat
Birkhäuser, Basel 2002

Mies van der Rohe – IIT Campus
Birkhäuser, Basel 2002

Helmut Jahn
Architecture /Engineering
Birkhäuser, Basel 2002

Helmut Jahn
Bayer Konzernzentrale /
Bayer Headquarter
Birkhäuser, Basel 2003

Eduardo Souto de Moura
Element Stein /Element Stone
Birkhäuser, Basel 2003

Gene Summers – Art /Architecture
Birkhäuser, Basel 2003

Helmut Jahn, Werner Sobek,
Matthias Schuler
Post Tower Bonn
Birkhäuser, Basel 2004

Innen-Hof in Marrakesch /
Courtyards in Marrakech
Birkhäuser, Basel 2004

Theo Hotz
Weishaupt Brenner und Heizsysteme
Niggli, Sulgen 2004

Mies van der Rohe
Federal Center Chicago
Birkhäuser, Basel 2004

Wilhelm Münger
Geist im Holz /Spirit of wood
Reinhardt, Basel 2004

Helmut Jahn
State Street Village IIT
Flash Press, Chicago 2004

Jakob Schilling – Planen Bauen
Sturm, Muttenz 2005

Renzo Piano – Zentrum Paul Klee
erschienen auf deutsch,
französisch, englisch /published in
German, French, English
Reinhardt, Basel 2005

Tadao Ando – Nähe des Fernen /
The Nearness of the Distant
Niggli, Sulgen 2005

Werner Blaser
Passion eines Lebens /
Passion of a Life
Sturm, Muttenz 2006

Tadao Ando
Bauen in die Erde /Sunken Courts
Niggli, Sulgen 2007

Archi Swiss
Parallelen mit der Grossen Welt
Regent, Basel 2009

Im Garten Isfahan /
In the Garden of Isfahan
Niggli, Sulgen 2009

Kurzbiografie von Werner Blaser

1924	Geboren am 29. August in Basel
1942–1946	Lehre als Möbelschreiner in Basel
1947–1948	Hospitant an der Kunstgewerbeschule Basel
1949–1951	Praktikant bei Alvar Aalto in Helsinki
1951–1953	Studium am Illinois Institute of Technology in Chicago (The Institute of Design)
1953	Recherchen zu den klassischen Tempel- und Teehäuser in Japan
1956–1957	Gastdozent an der Hochschule für Gestaltung in Ulm
1963–1964	Arbeit am Buch *Kunst der Struktur* mit Mies van der Rohe in Chicago
1978	Gastprofessor University of Philadelphia (USA)
1980–2003	Basler Architekturvorträge
1982–1983	Gastprofessor Universität für angewandte Kunst Wien

Mitgliedschaften

SWB	Schweizer Werkbund seit 1956
BDA	Korrespondierendes Mitglied Bund Deutscher Architekten seit 1973
REG	Eintragung in das Schweizer Register als Architekt 1973
SIA	Schweizerischer Ingenieur- und Architektenverein seit 1973
BSA	Bund Schweizer Architekten seit 1974

Ausstellungen

– *Alvar Aalto*, in den Räumen Baldwin Kingrey, Chicago 1950
– *Tempel und Teehaus in Japan*, Gewerbemuseum Basel 1955 *(Katalog)*
– *Neue Möbel von Werner Blaser*, Wohnbedarf Basel 1958
– *Architektur bis ins Möbel – Werner Blaser Design*, Universität für angewandte Kunst Wien *(Katalog)*
– *Der Fels ist mein Haus*, Ciba-Geigy, Basel 1976
– *Werner Blaser – Prinzip einer Architektur*, Bündner Kunstmuseum Chur 1977 *(Katalog)*
– *China Hofhäuser*, Kunstgewerbemuseum Zürich 1979 *(Katalog)*
– *Mies van der Rohe – Parallelen*, Suter + Suter, Basel 1987 *(Katalog)*

Wanderausstellungen

– *Möbel in Holz und Stahl, Alvar Aalto* – Mies van der Rohe, Gewerbemuseum Basel / Die Neue Sammlung München 1958 *(Katalog)*
– *Beispiel Japan, Bau und Gerät*, Kunstgewerbemuseum Zürich / Bayerische Akademie der Schönen Künste München 1965
– *Objektive Architektur – Beispiel «Skin and Skeleton»*, Die neue Sammlung, München / Gewerbemuseum Basel 1973 *(Faltblatt)*
– *Strukturale Architektur aus Osteuropa*, Gewerbemuseum Basel / Technische Hochschule Antwerpen 1975
– *70/80 Architecture Switzerland*, Kunsthalle Basel 1981 und in weiteren 90 Städten weltweit *(Buch)*

– *Mies van der Rohe – less is more*, eine Ausstellung in Aachen, Tokio, Weimar 1986 *(Faltblatt)*
– *West meets East / Mies van der Rohe*, Mies' Landhaus Lemke, Berlin 1999 / Architekturmuseum Helsinki 2000 / Bauhaus Universität Weimar 2002

Tätigkeit im Design

– «Good Design» (Auszeichnung) vom Museum of Modern Art New York 1953
– Erster und ex aequo Preise, Concorso Internazionale del Mobile Cantù, Italien, 1955 und 1961
– Stahlrohrsessel «all in line» für Josef Albers aus einem Element, 1958
– Kletterlabyrinth für Kindergarten in Basel 1960
– Wohnungseinrichtung Expo 64 in Lausanne 1963–1964
– Kindergarten Christoph Merian Stiftung, Basel 1966–1967
– Klappbarer Holzsessel, 1973–1977
– Einfachmöbel im Paket, 1975–1977

Architektur

– Friedhofanlage Bromhübel in Arlesheim, Basel-Landschaft (Planer: Baumann, Blaser, Schilling, Seiberth) 1960–1967
– Demontabler Ausstellungspavillon Ciba-Photochemie in Köln 1962–1963
– Kinderdorf Müllheim, Baden-Württemberg (Architekten: Werner Blaser, Nees & Beutler) 1963–1967
– Sozialpädagogische Sonderschule mit Heim, Kinderheim Tüllinger Höhe, Baden-Württemberg, Projekt 1966–1973 (Bebauungsplan)
– Wohnhäuser in Stahlskelett in Bottmingen, Basel-Landschaft 1968–1969
– Kirchgemeindehaus mit Pfarrwohnung und Kindergarten in Neuenburg, Baden-Württemberg
– Lagerhalle mit Büro in Raumfachwerk, J. Lüber in Märkt, Baden-Württemberg 1970–1971
– Sechseckhäuser in Holzskelett in Biel- Benken und im Berner Jura 1972–1973
– Renovation und Pergola der Casa Nascosta in Ancona 1976–1977
– Einrichtung Birkhäuser Verlag in Therwil 1982
– Kindergarten-Pavillon in Bottmingen 1986

Studienreisen

Skandinavien, England, Griechenland (Sifnos), Irland (Aran-Inseln), Deutschland (Weimar und Dessau), Russland (Onegasee und Tomsk, Sibirien), Rumänien (Maramureş), Bulgarien, USA (New York, Chicago, Los Angeles), Kuba, Argentinien, Brasilien, Ägypten, Saudi-Arabien, Marokko, Marrakesch, Iran (Isfahan), Japan, China, Indien (Rajasthan), Frankreich (Neukaledonien), Finnland, 1949–2010.

Werner Blaser – Short Biography

1924	Born on 29 August in Basel, Switzerland
1942–1946	Trained as furniture maker in Basel
1947–1948	Guest student at the Basel College of the Arts
1949–1951	Trainee at Alvar Aalto in Helsinki
1951–1953	Studied at the Illinois Institute of Technology in Chicago (The Institute of Design)
1953	Studied classic temple and teahouse construction in Japan
1956–1957	Guest professor at the Academy of Design in Ulm, Germany
1963–1964	Work on the book *Kunst der Struktur* (Art of Structure) with Mies van der Rohe in Chicago
1978	Guest professor at Philadelphia University
1980–2003	Lectures on architecture in Basel
1982–1983	Guest professor at the University of Applied Arts, Vienna

Professional memberships

SWB	Swiss Federation of Architects, Artists, Builders, since 1956
BDA	Corresponding member of the Association of German Architects, since 1973
REG	Entry in the Swiss Registry as architect, 1973
SIA	Association of Swiss Engineers and Architects, since 1973
BSA	Association of Swiss Architects, since 1974

Exhibitions

- *Alvar Aalto,* in the Baldwin Kingrey rooms, Chicago, 1950
- *Temple and Teahouse in Japan,* Basel School of Applied Arts, 1955 *(catalogue)*
- *New Furniture by Werner Blaser,* Wohnbedarf Basel, 1958
- *From Architecture to Furniture – Werner Blaser Design,* University of Applied Arts, Vienna *(catalogue)*
- *The Rock Is My House,* Ciba-Geigy, Basel, 1976
- *Werner Blaser – Concept of an Architecture,* Bündner Kunstmuseum, Chur, Switzerland, 1977 *(catalogue)*
- *Chinese Courtyard Houses,* Kunstgewerbemuseum Zürich, 1979 *(catalogue)*
- *Mies van der Rohe – Parallels,* Suter + Suter, Basel, 1987 *(catalogue)*

Traveling exhibitions

- *Furniture in Wood and Steel, Alvar Aalto* – Mies van der Rohe, Gewerbemuseum Basel / Die Neue Sammlung, Munich, 1958 *(catalogue)*
- *Japan as Model, Building and Machinery,* Kunstgewerbemuseum Zürich / Bayerische Akademie der Schönen Künste, Munich, 1965
- *Objective Architecture – "Skin and Skeleton" Model,* Die neue Sammlung, Munich / Gewerbemuseum Basel, 1973 *(leaflet)*
- *Structural Architecture from Eastern Europe,* Gewerbemuseum Basel / Technical Academy of Antwerp, 1975
- *70/80 Architecture Switzerland,* Kunsthalle Basel 1981 and worldwide in 90 cities *(book)*

- *Mies van der Rohe – less is more,* an exhibition in Aachen, Tokyo, Weimar, 1986 *(leaflet)*
- *West Meets East/Mies van der Rohe,* Mies' Landhaus Lemke, Berlin, 1999 / Architekturmuseum Helsinki 2000 / Bauhaus Universität Weimar, 2002

Design work

- Good Design Award, Museum of Modern Art, New York, 1953
- First and ex aequo awards, Concorso Internazionale del Mobile Cantù, Italy, 1955 and 1961
- Steel pipe chair "all in line" for Josef Albers from a single element, 1958
- Climbing maze for kindergarten in Basel, 1960
- Apartment interior, Expo 64 in Lausanne, Switzerland, 1963–1964
- Christoph Merian Stiftung kindergarten, Basel, 1966–1967
- Foldable wood chair, 1973–197
- Einfachmöbel im Paket, 1975–1977

Architecture

- Bromhübel cemetery facility in Arlesheim, Basel-Landschaft, Switzerland (Planner: Baumann, Blaser, Schilling, Seiberth), 1960–1967
- Demountable Ciba photochemistry exhibition pavilion in Cologne, 1962–1963
- Müllheim Children's Village, Baden-Württemberg, Germany (Architects: Werner Blaser, Nees & Beutler), 1963–1967
- Special needs school facility with dormitory, Tüllinger Höhe Children's Home, Baden-Württemberg, Germany, 1966–1973 project (development plan)
- Steel frame residential buildings in Bottmingen, Basel-Landschaft, 1968–1969
- Parish community house with priest's private apartment and kindergarten in Neuenburg, Baden-Württemberg, Germany
- Warehouse with office in space frame, J. Lüber in Märkt, Baden-Württemberg, Germany, 1970–1971
- Six-sided buildings with wooden frame in Biel-Benken and Bernese Jura, Switzerland, 1972–1973
- Renovation and pergola of Casa Nascosta in Ancona, Italy, 1976–1977
- Interior of the Birkhäuser publishing house in Therwil, Switzerland, 1982
- Kindergarten pavilion in Bottmingen, Switzerland, 1986

Study-related travel

Scandinavia, England, Greece (Sifnos), Ireland (Aran Islands), Germany (Weimar and Dessau), Russia (Lake Onega and Tomsk, Siberia), Rumania (Maramureș), Bulgaria, United States (New York, Chicago, Los Angeles), Cuba, Argentina, Brazil, Egypt, Saudi Arabia, Morocco (Marrakech), Iran (Isfahan), Japan, China, India (Rajasthan), France (New Caledonia), Finland, 1949–2010.